HUE Coloring

TOUGH TIMES NEVER LAST
INSPIRATIONAL COLORING QUOTES

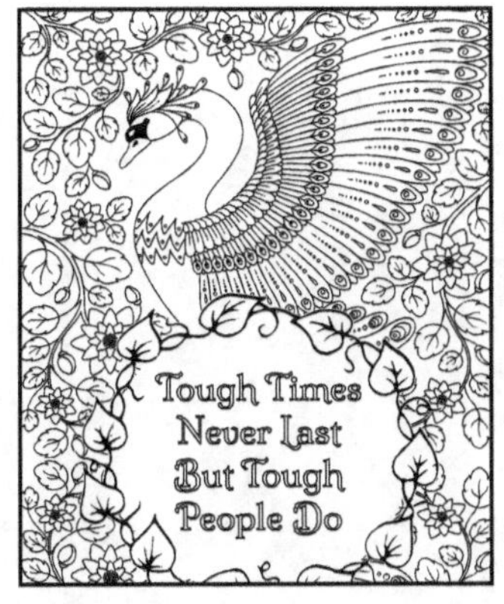

IN THIS COLORING BOOK...

50 Inspirational Quotes are included in this adult coloring book to help you relax and make your life more colorful. These illustrations are created for you to bring enjoyment to life, and designed with beautiful patterns that appeal
 to adult eyes.

TIPS TO A RELAXING COLORING

Find a quiet space. It's easier to focus on what you are doing when there
are no distractions.

Organize your materials. Lay out your coloring book and crayons, pens,
or pencils.

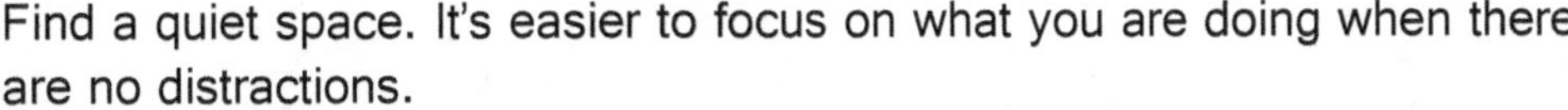

Set the mood. Turn on some tranquil music, diffuse lavender or another relaxing oil, and make sure you have your preferred drink at hand.

Select your picture. Which image speaks to you today? That's the one you should color. Choose your pallette. Select the colors you will be using for your image.

Begin coloring. This is the fun part. Don't worry about getting evrything perfect'
just start. If you feel you don't want to do it anymore, just stop!

SHOWS US YOUR CREATION!

We'd love to hear from you, show us what you created.
Facebook: www.facebook.com/huecoloring
Email: huecoloringbooks@gmail.com

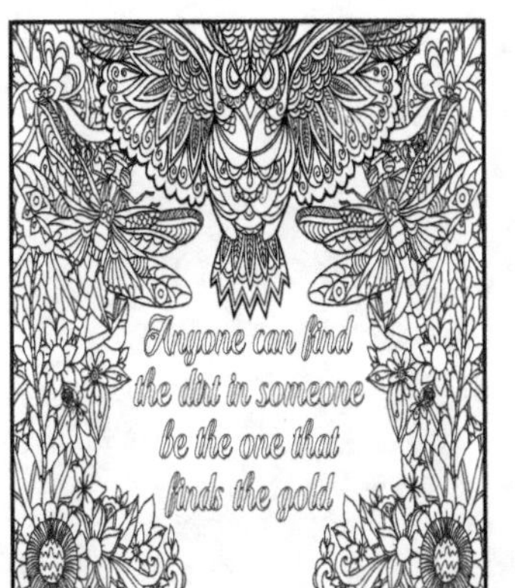

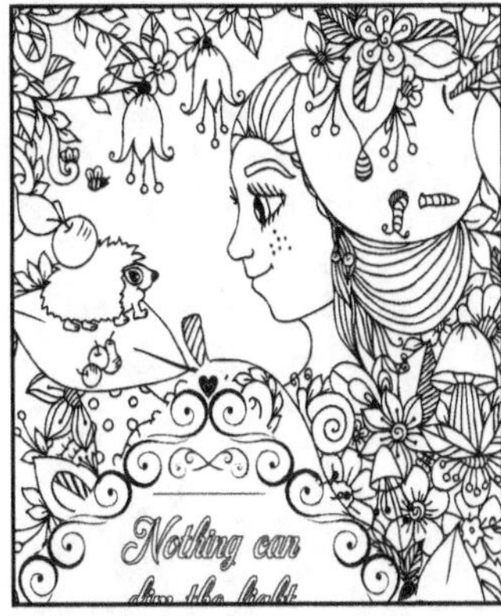

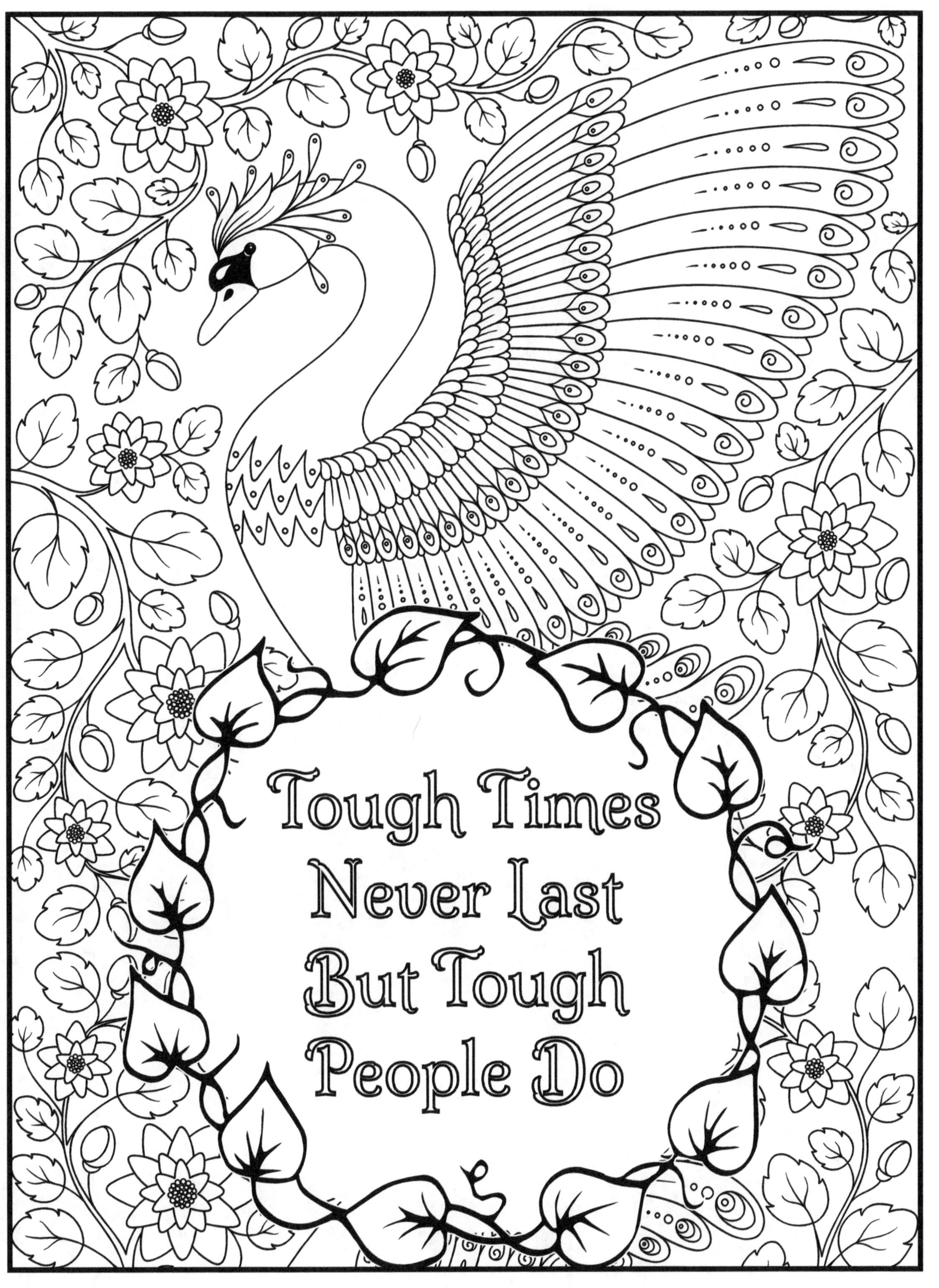

Tough Times
Never Last
But Tough
People Do

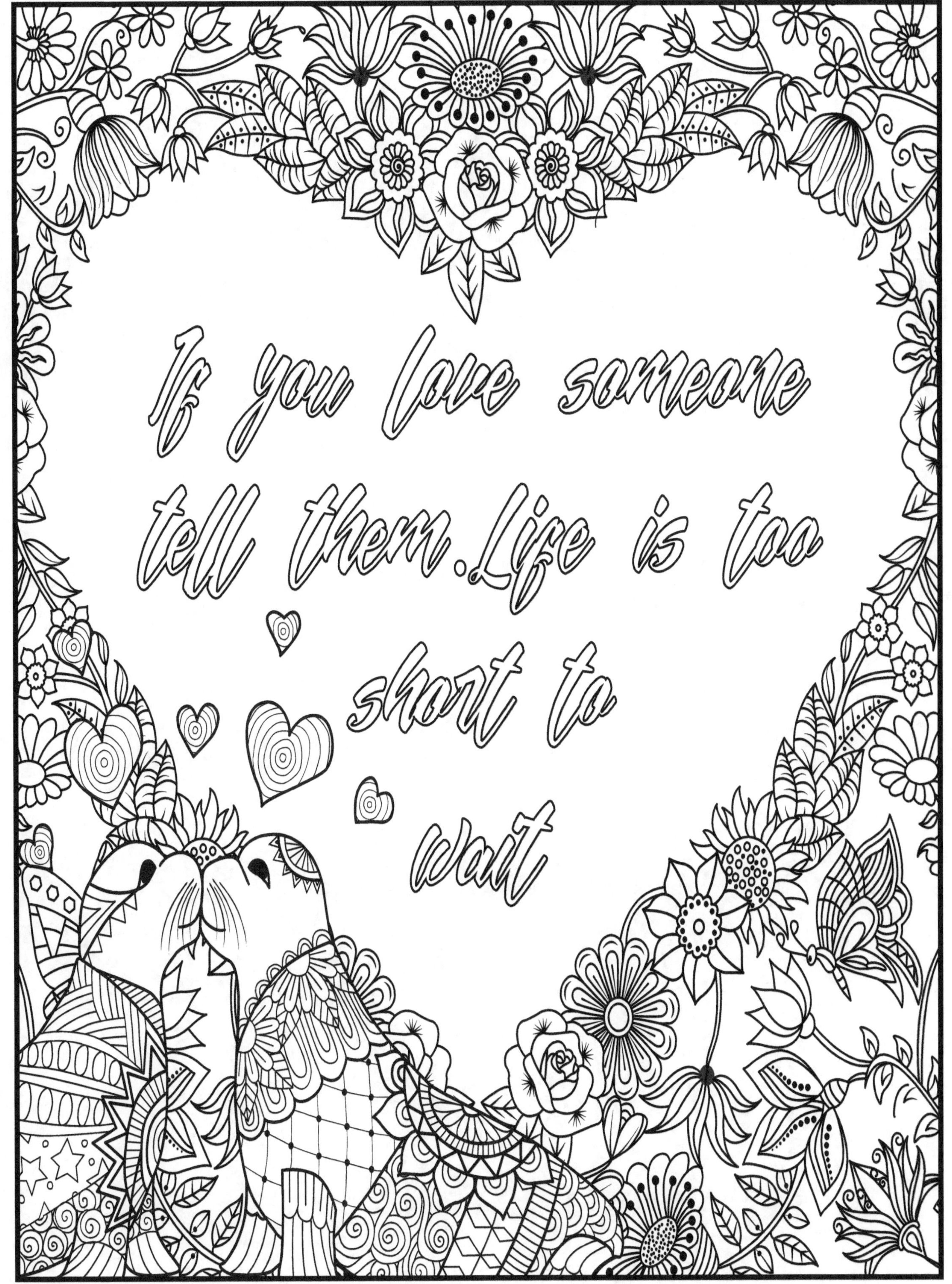

If you love someone
tell them. Life is too
short to
wait

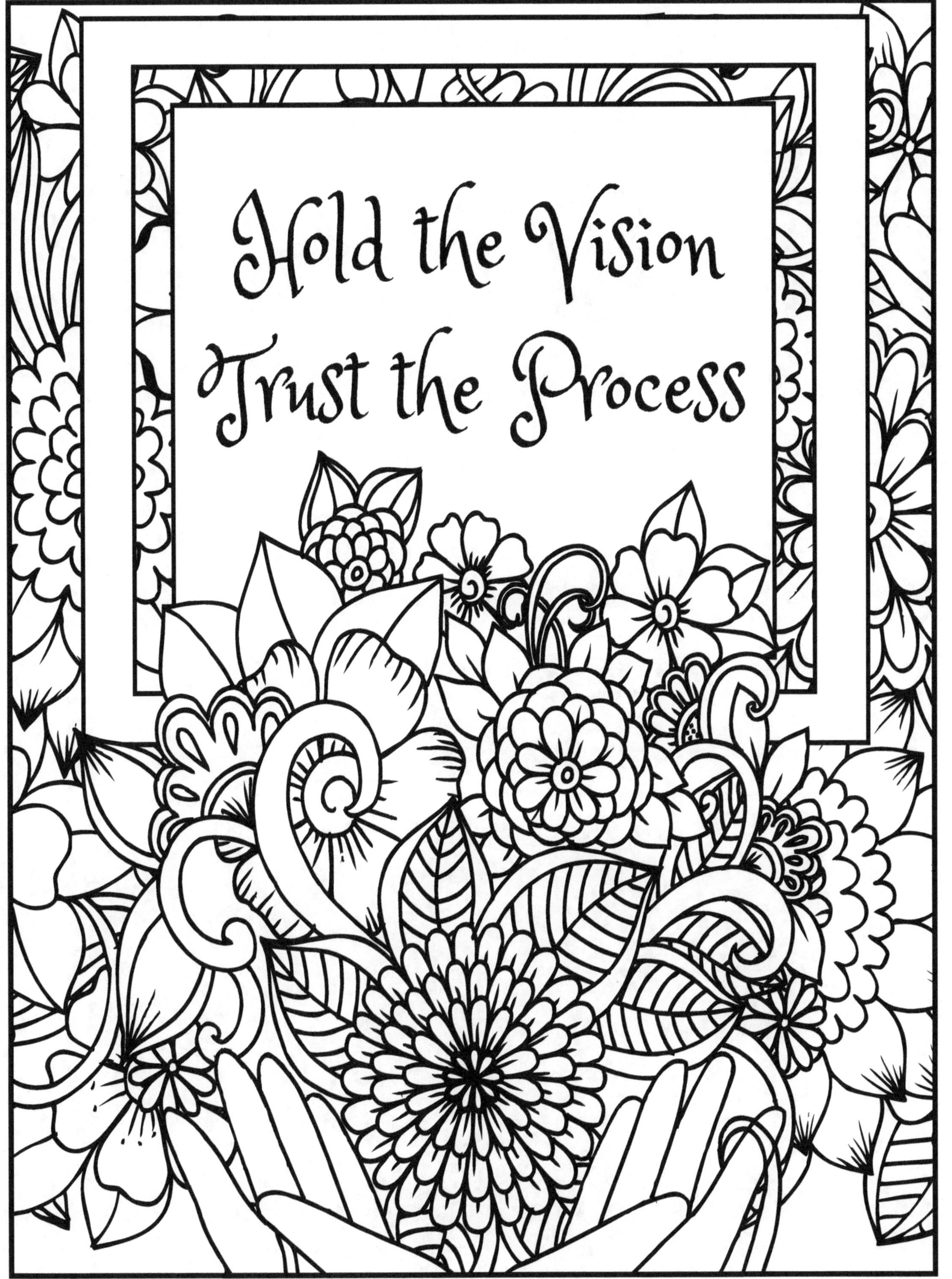
Hold the Vision
Trust the Process

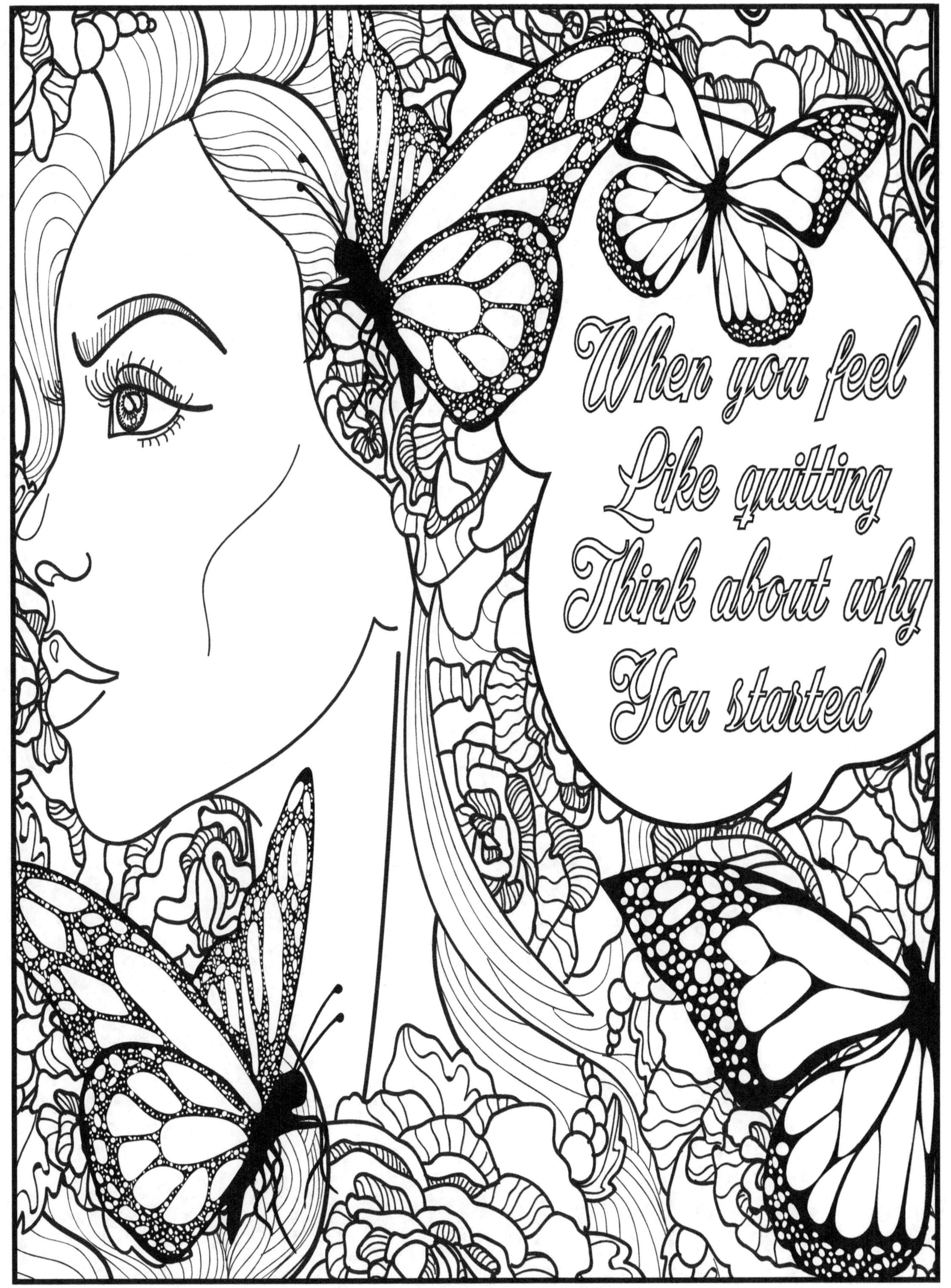

When you feel
Like quitting
Think about why
You started

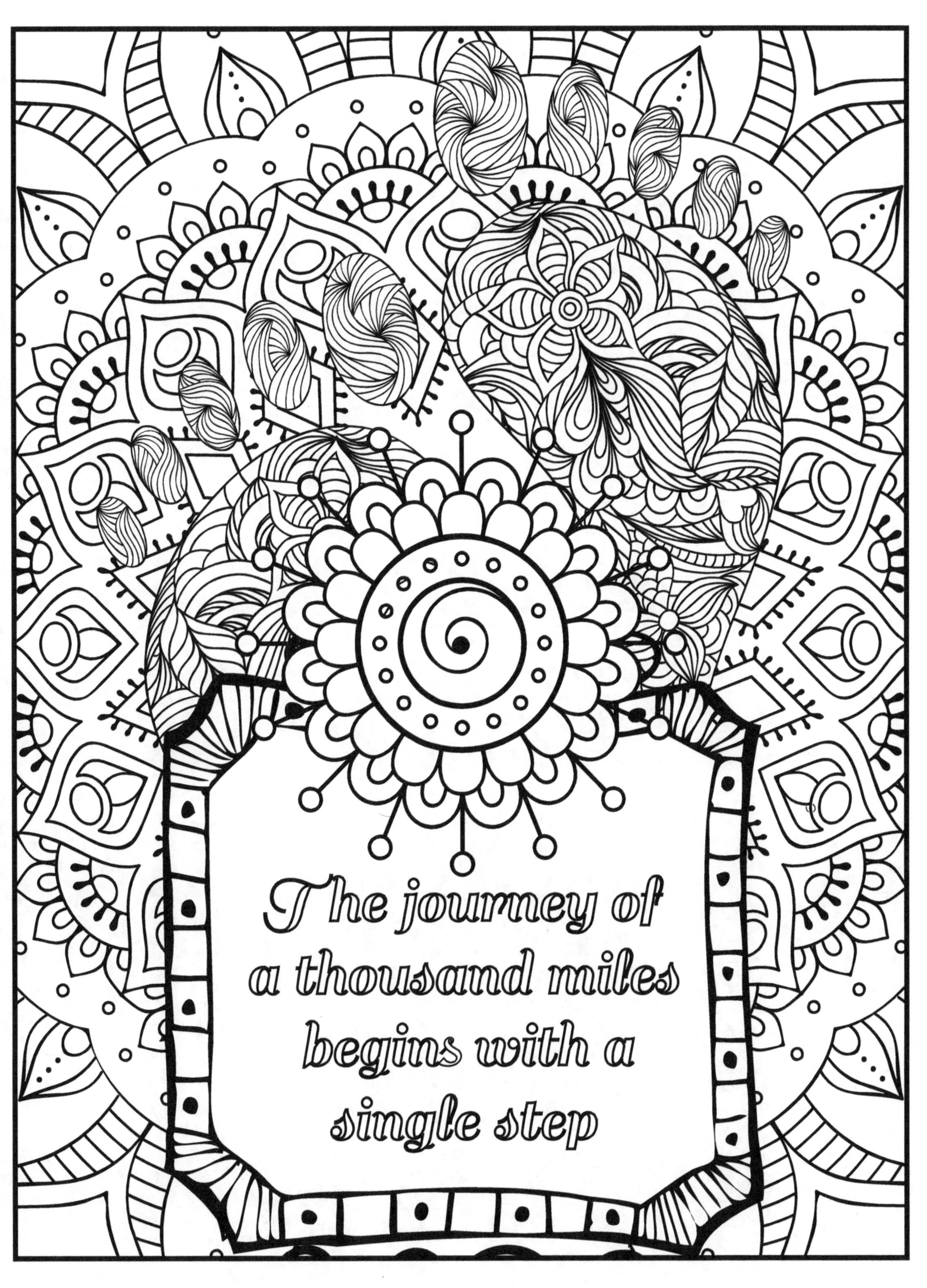

The journey of
a thousand miles
begins with a
single step

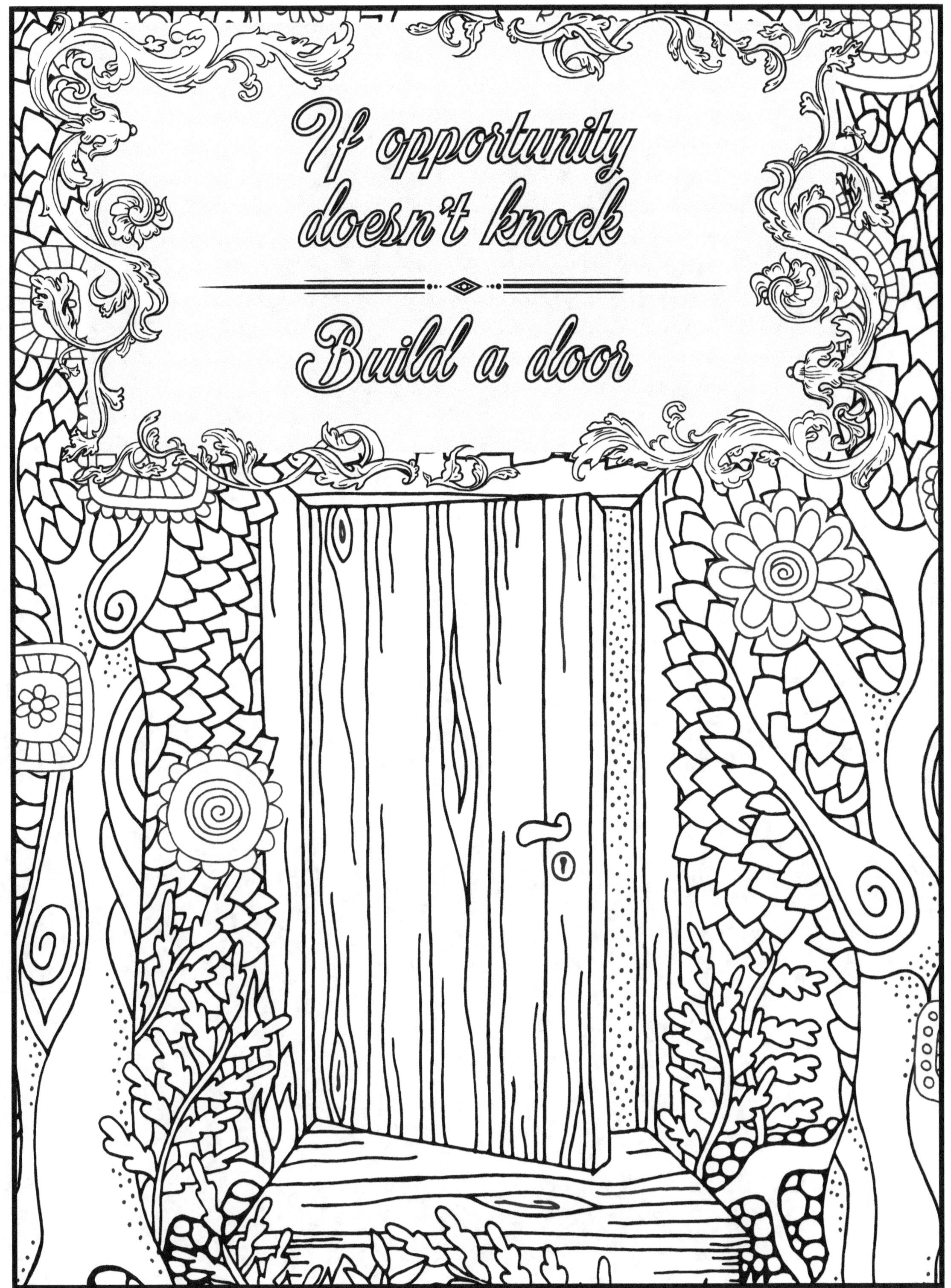

If opportunity
doesn't knock

Build a door

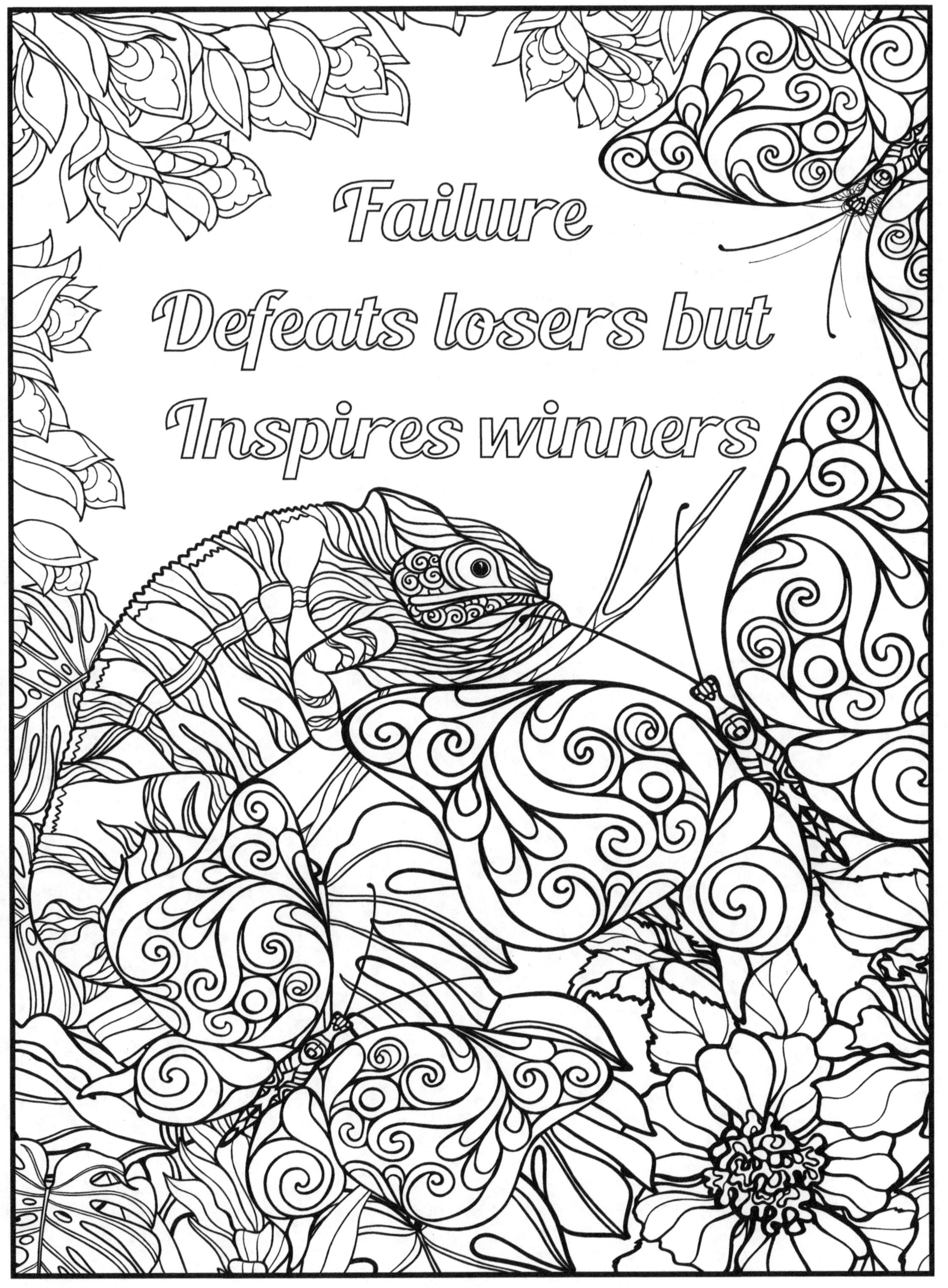

Failure
Defeats losers but
Inspires winners

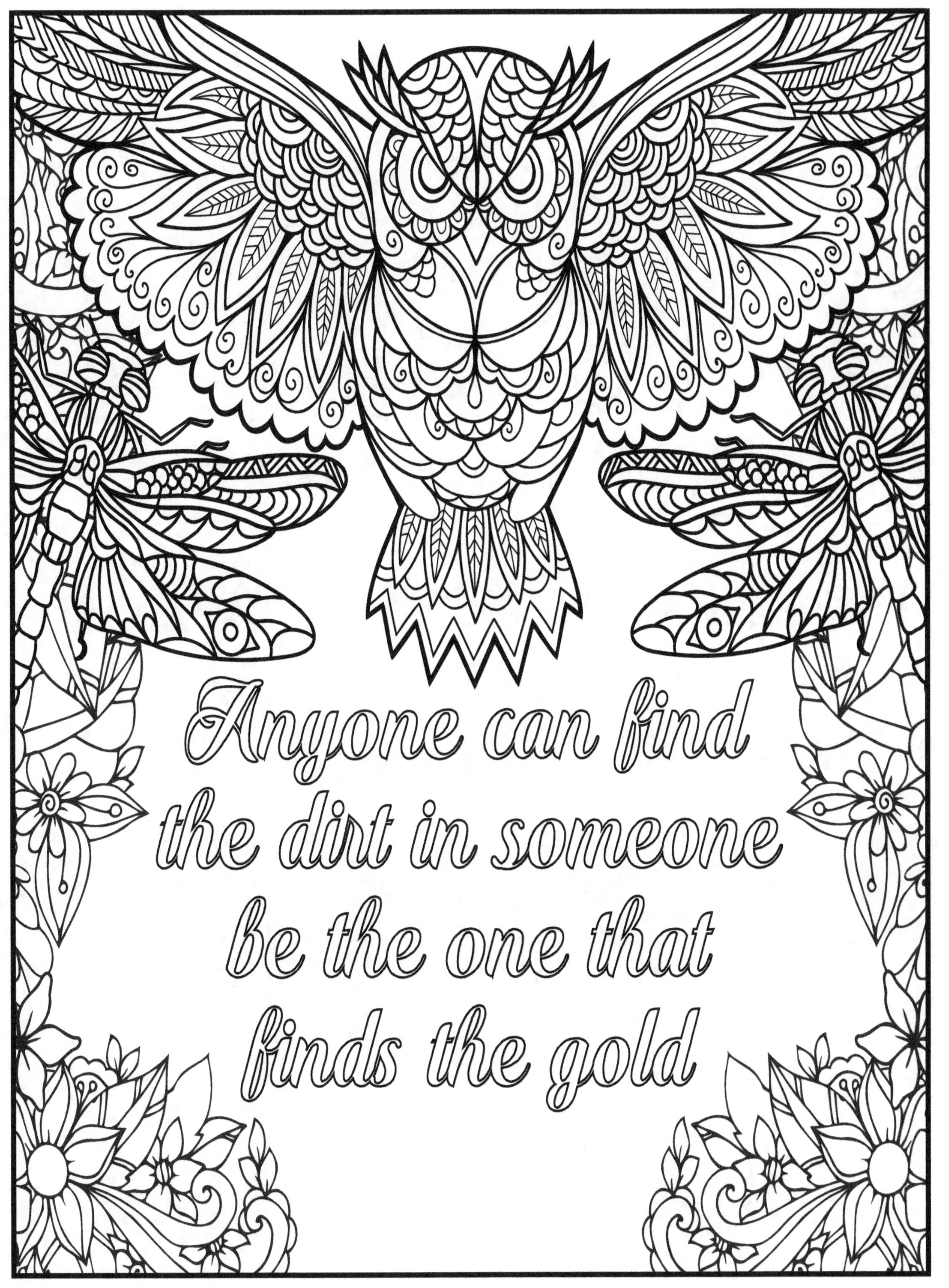
Anyone can find
the dirt in someone
be the one that
finds the gold

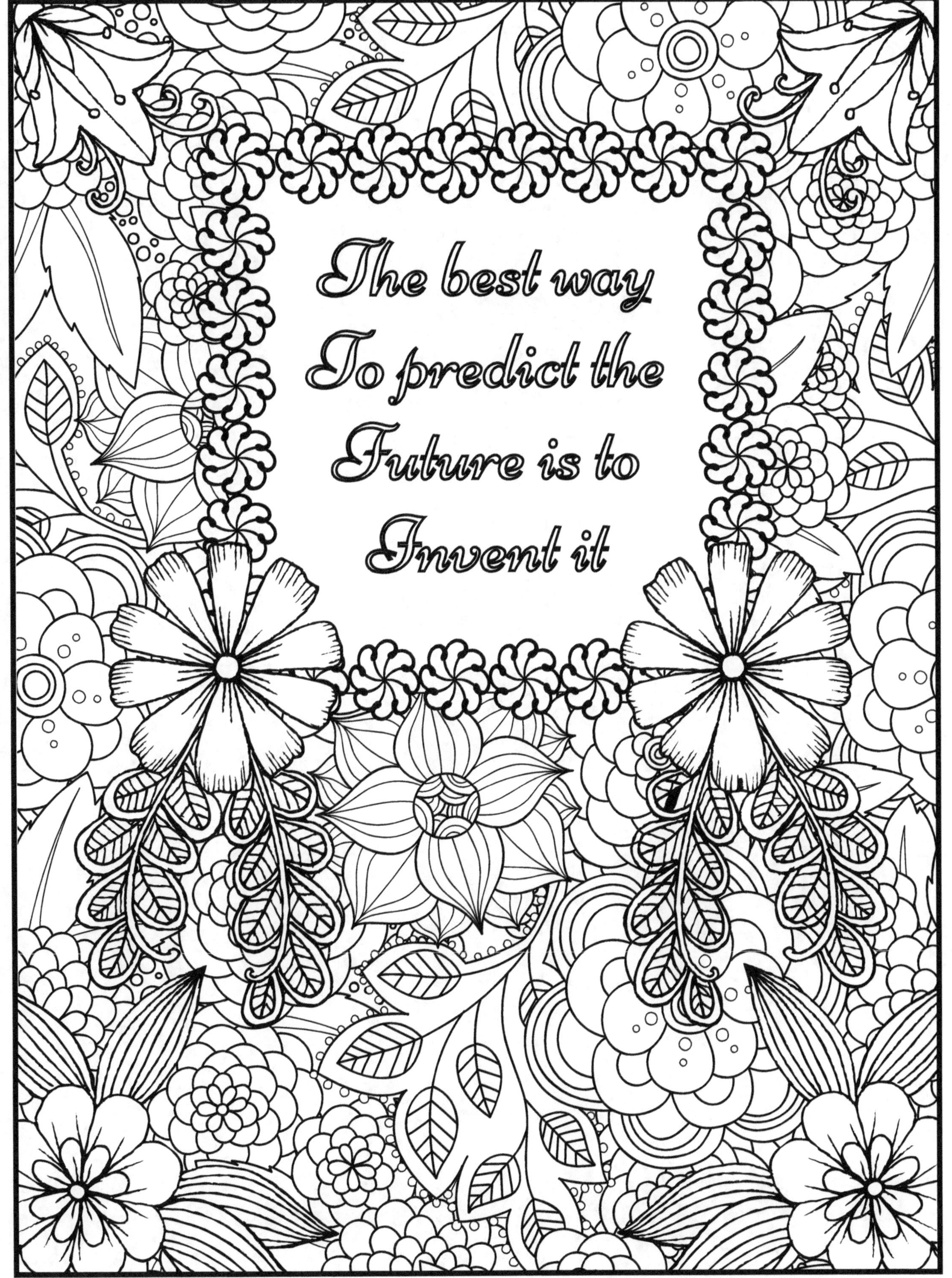

The best way
To predict the
Future is to
Invent it

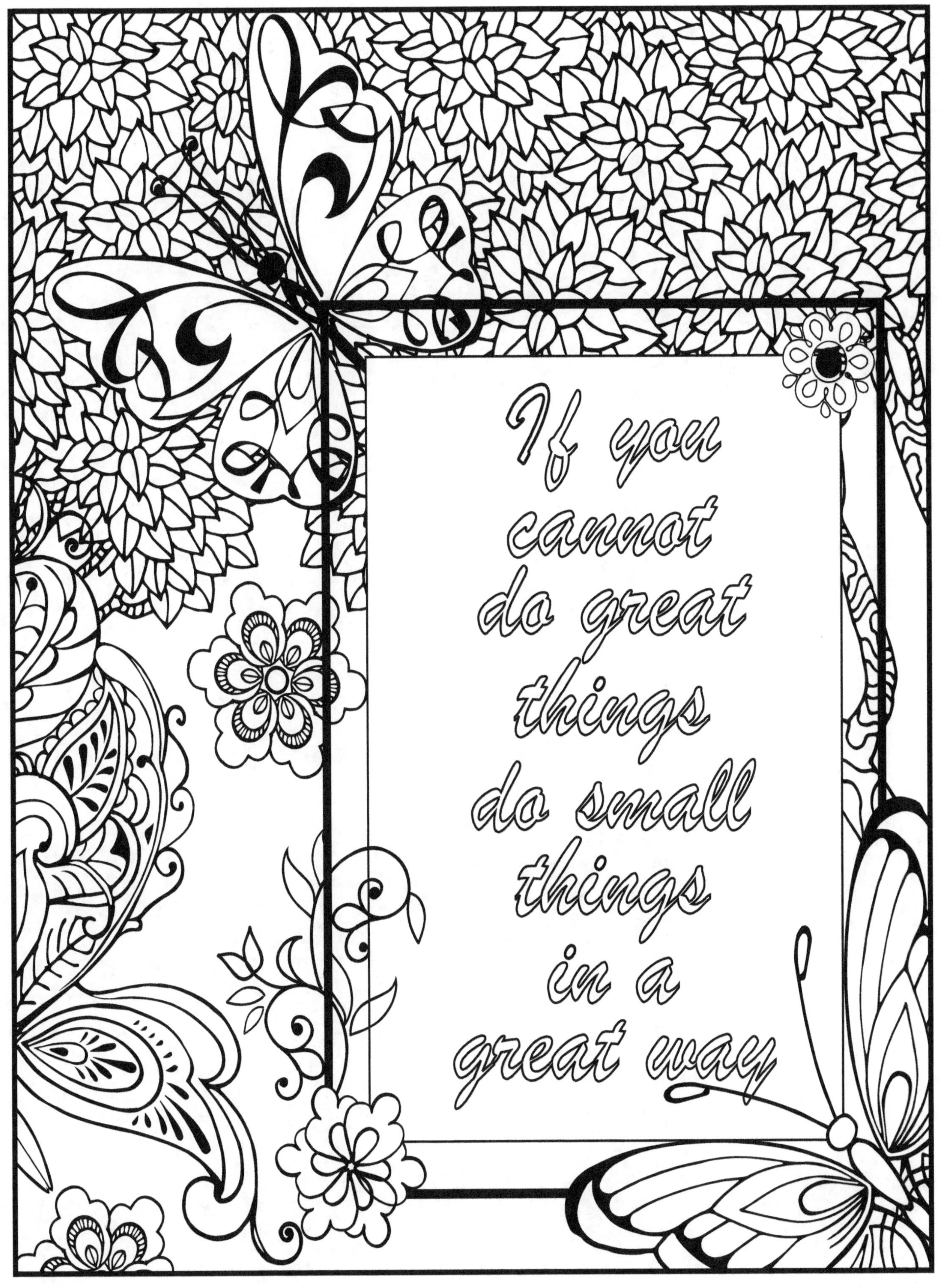
If you
cannot
do great
things
do small
things
in a
great way

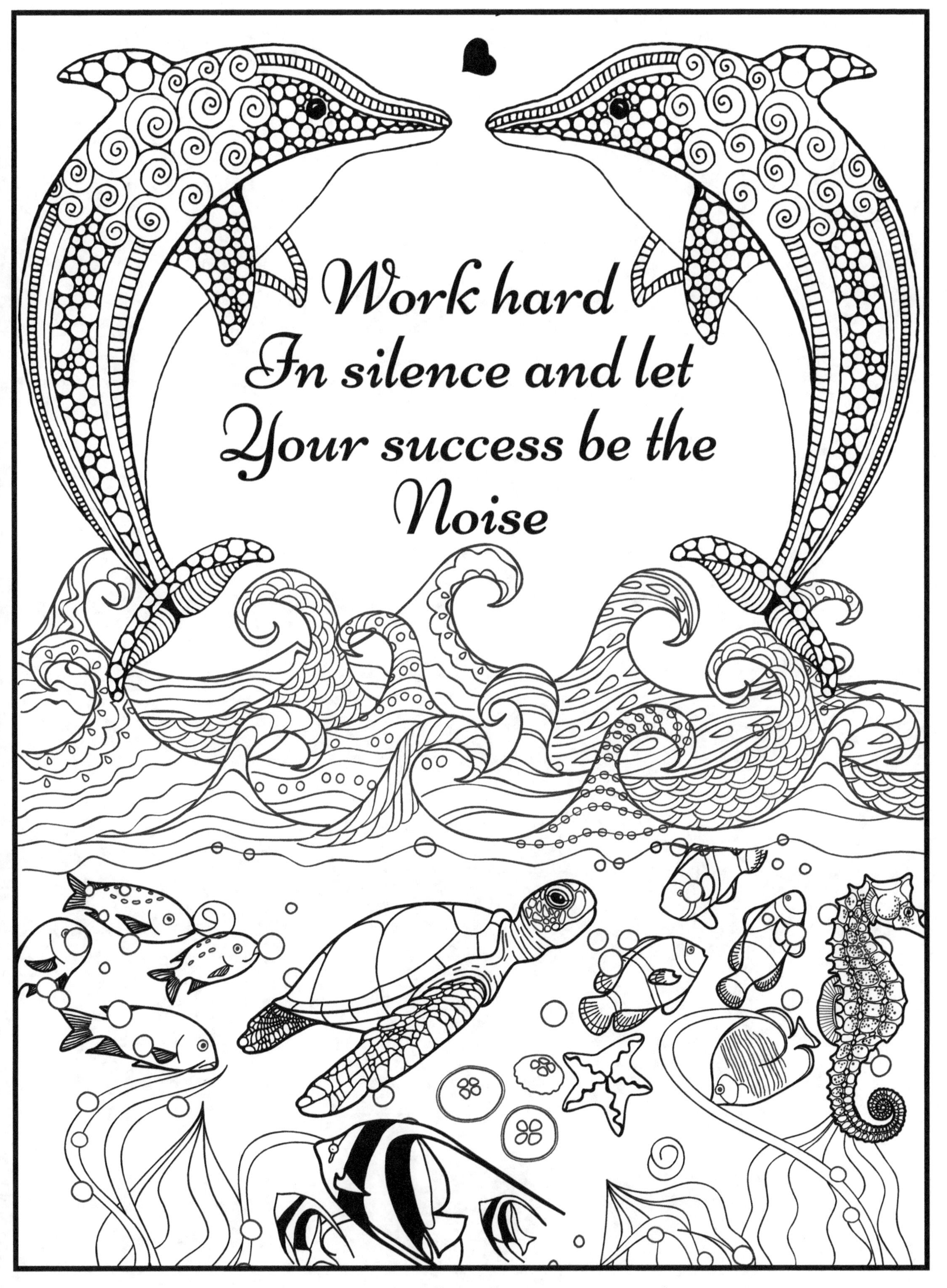

Work hard
In silence and let
Your success be the
Noise

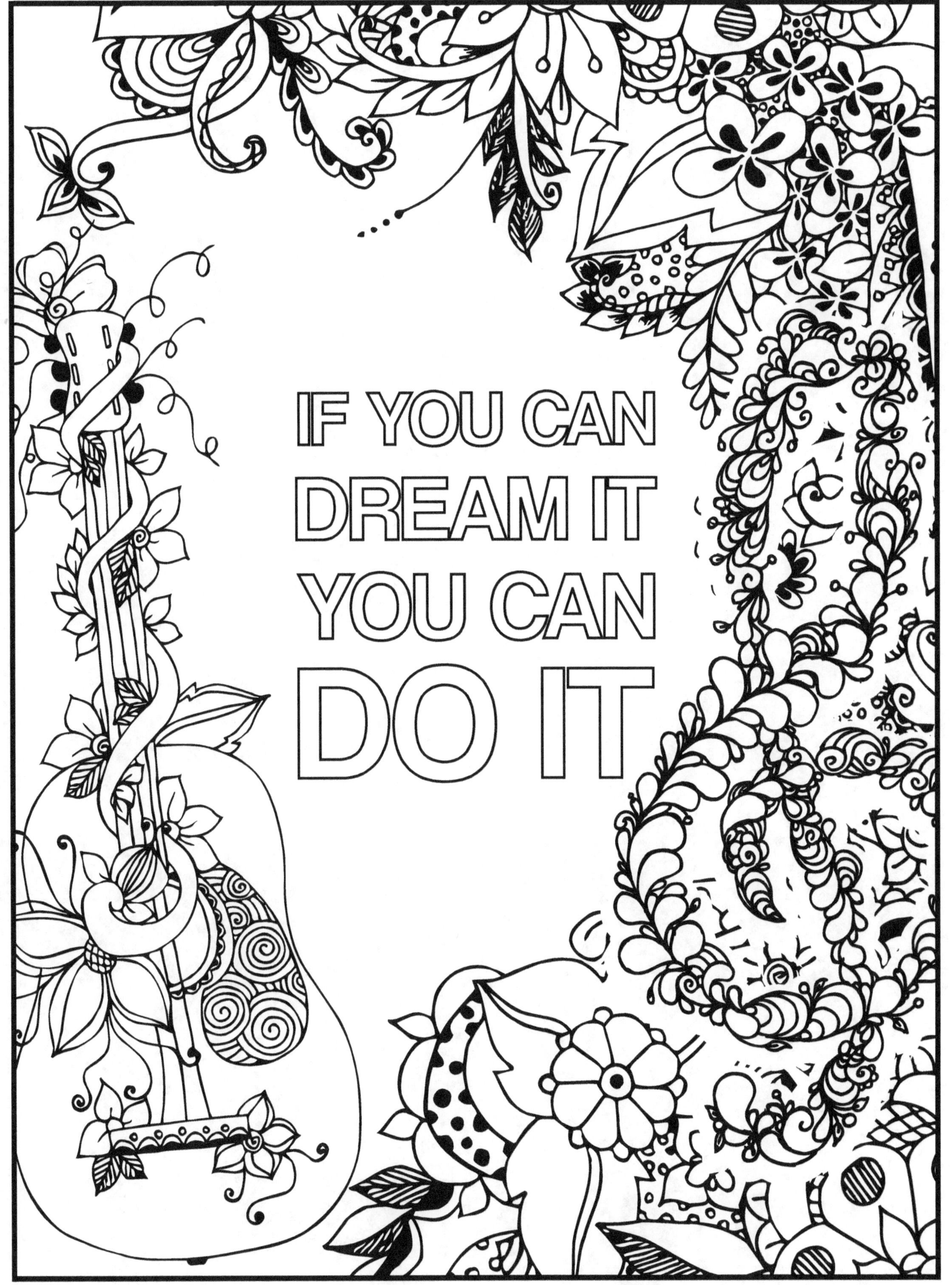

IF YOU CAN
DREAM IT
YOU CAN
DO IT

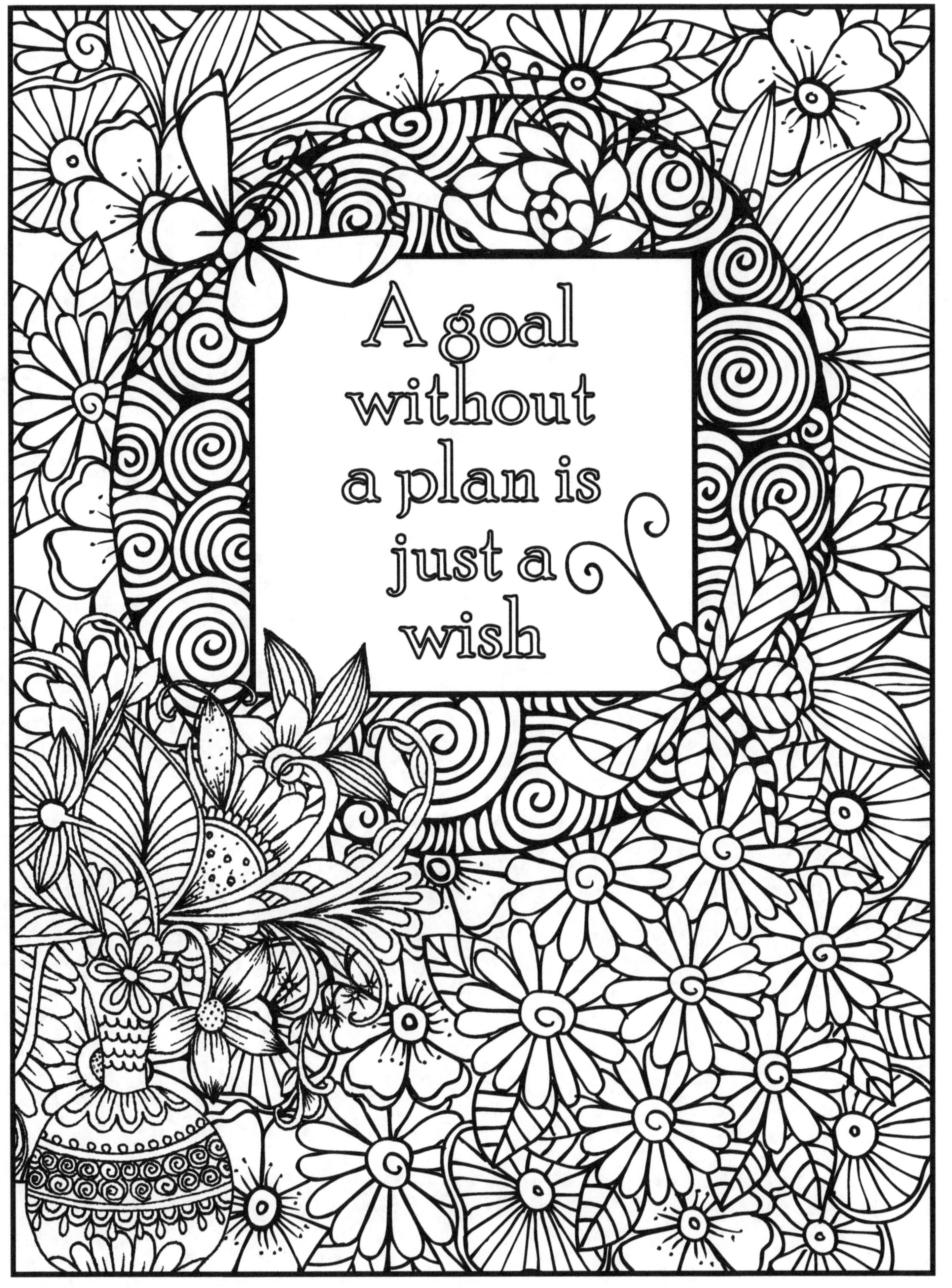

A goal
without
a plan is
just a
wish

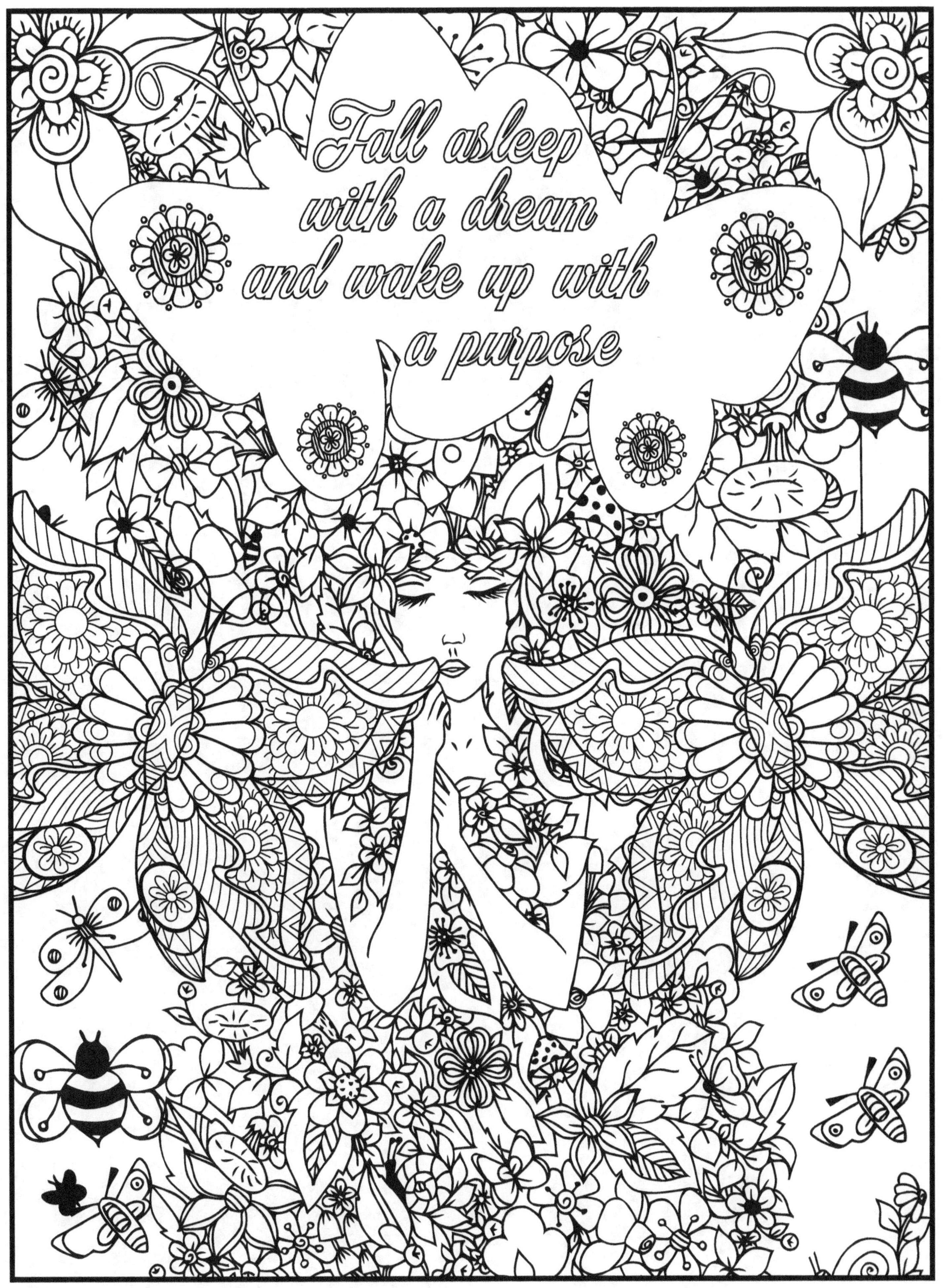

Fall asleep
with a dream
and wake up with
a purpose

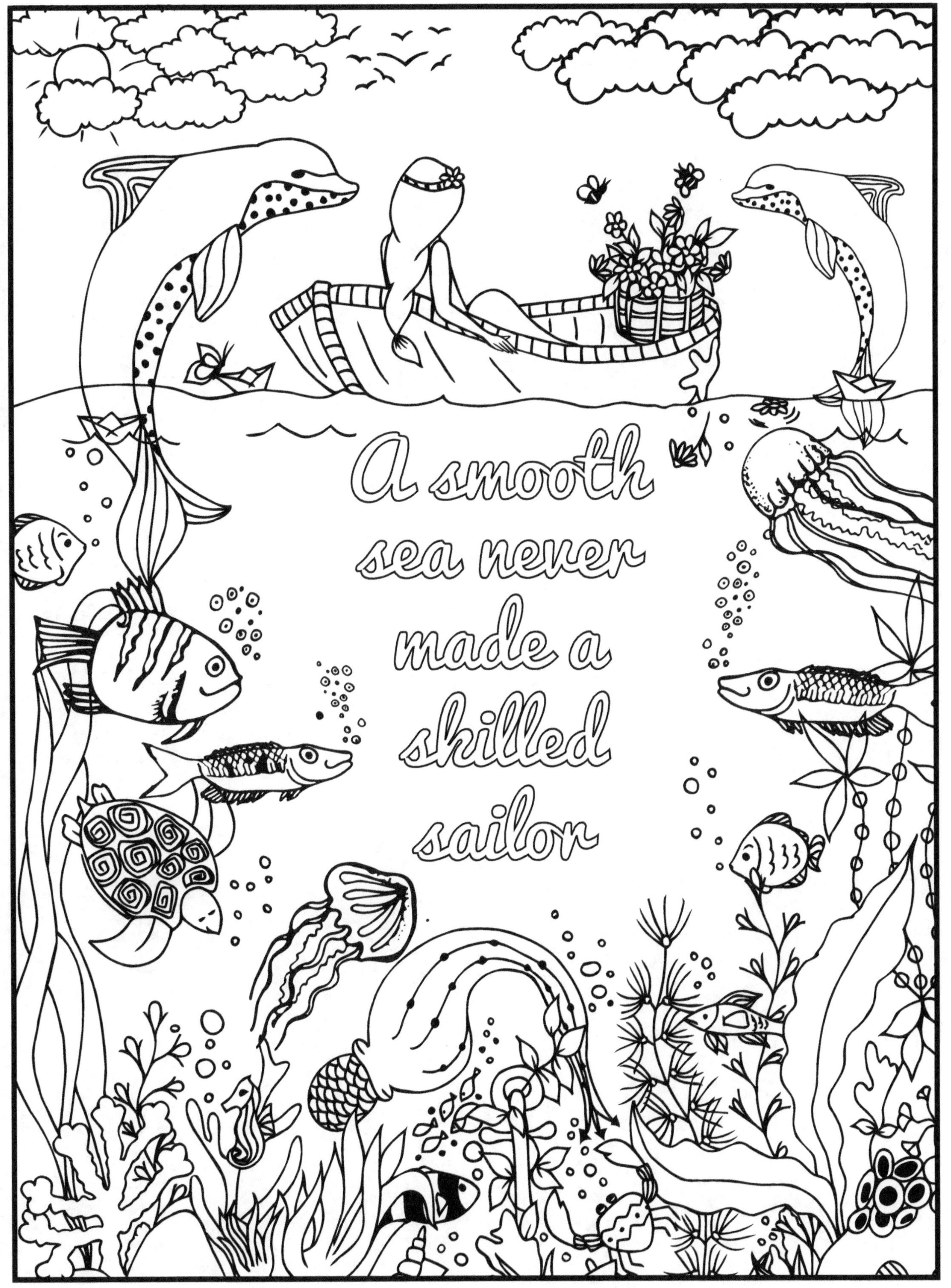

A smooth
sea never
made a
skilled
sailor

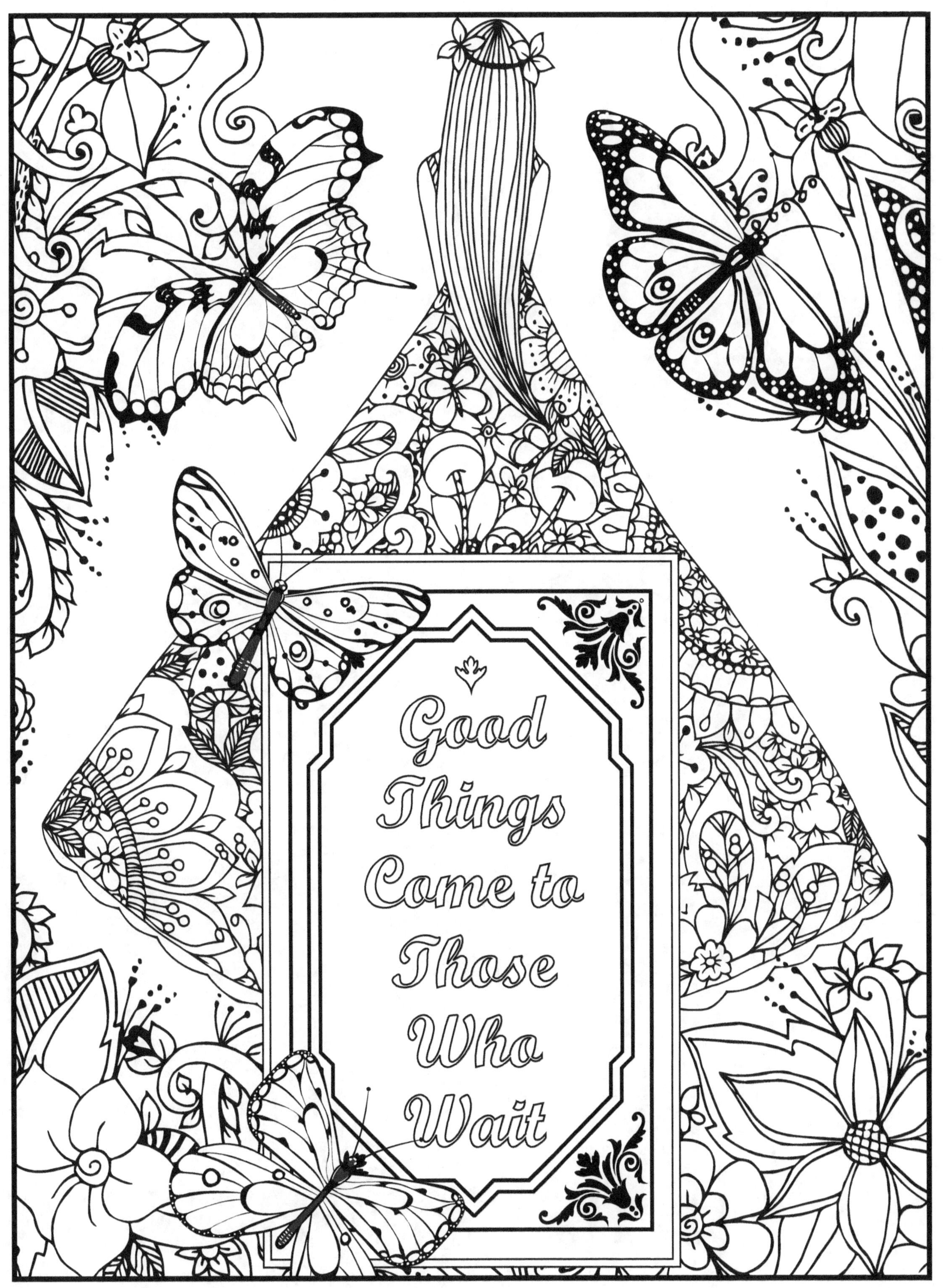
Good
Things
Come to
Those
Who
Wait

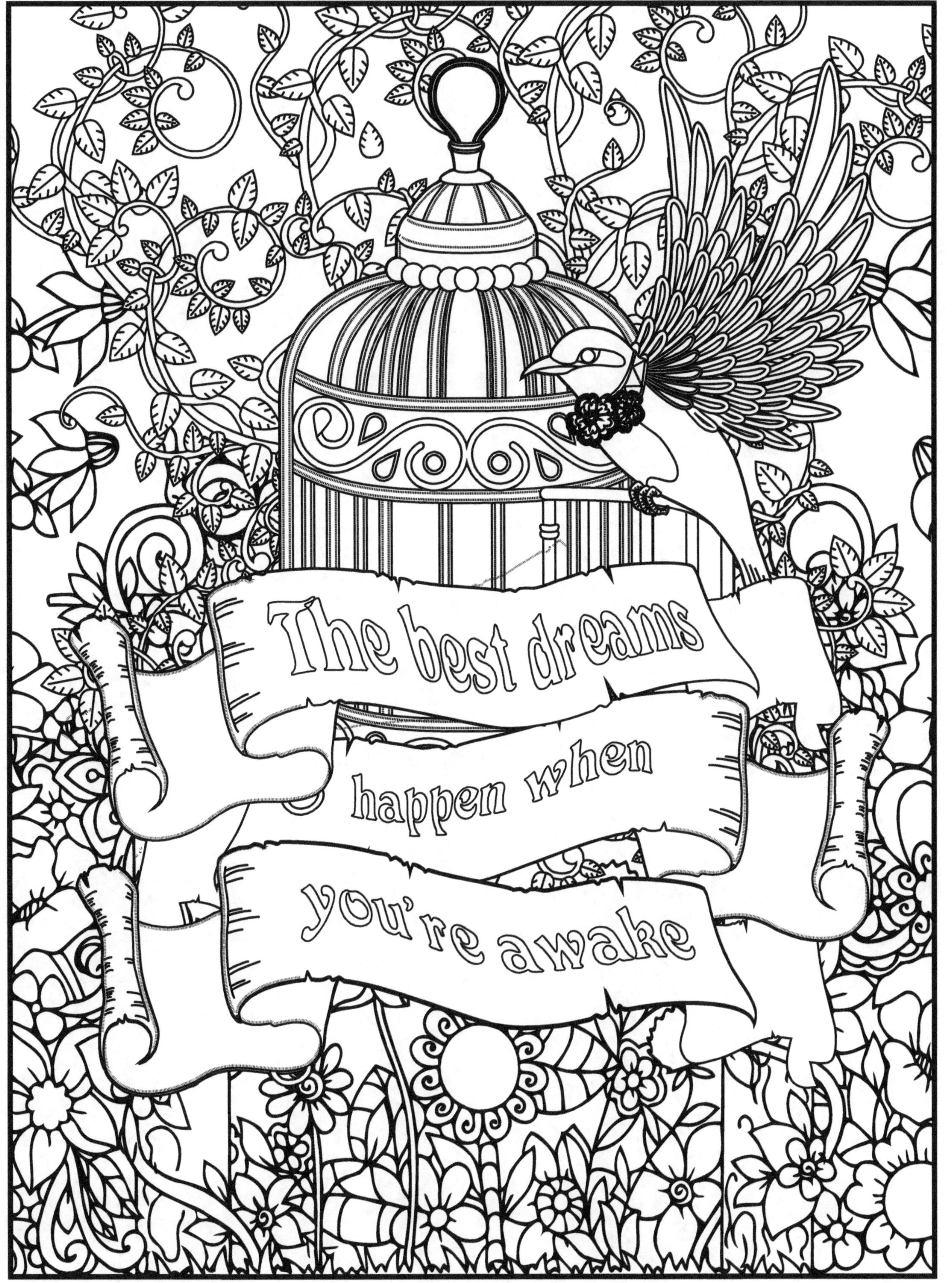

The best dreams
happen when
you're awake

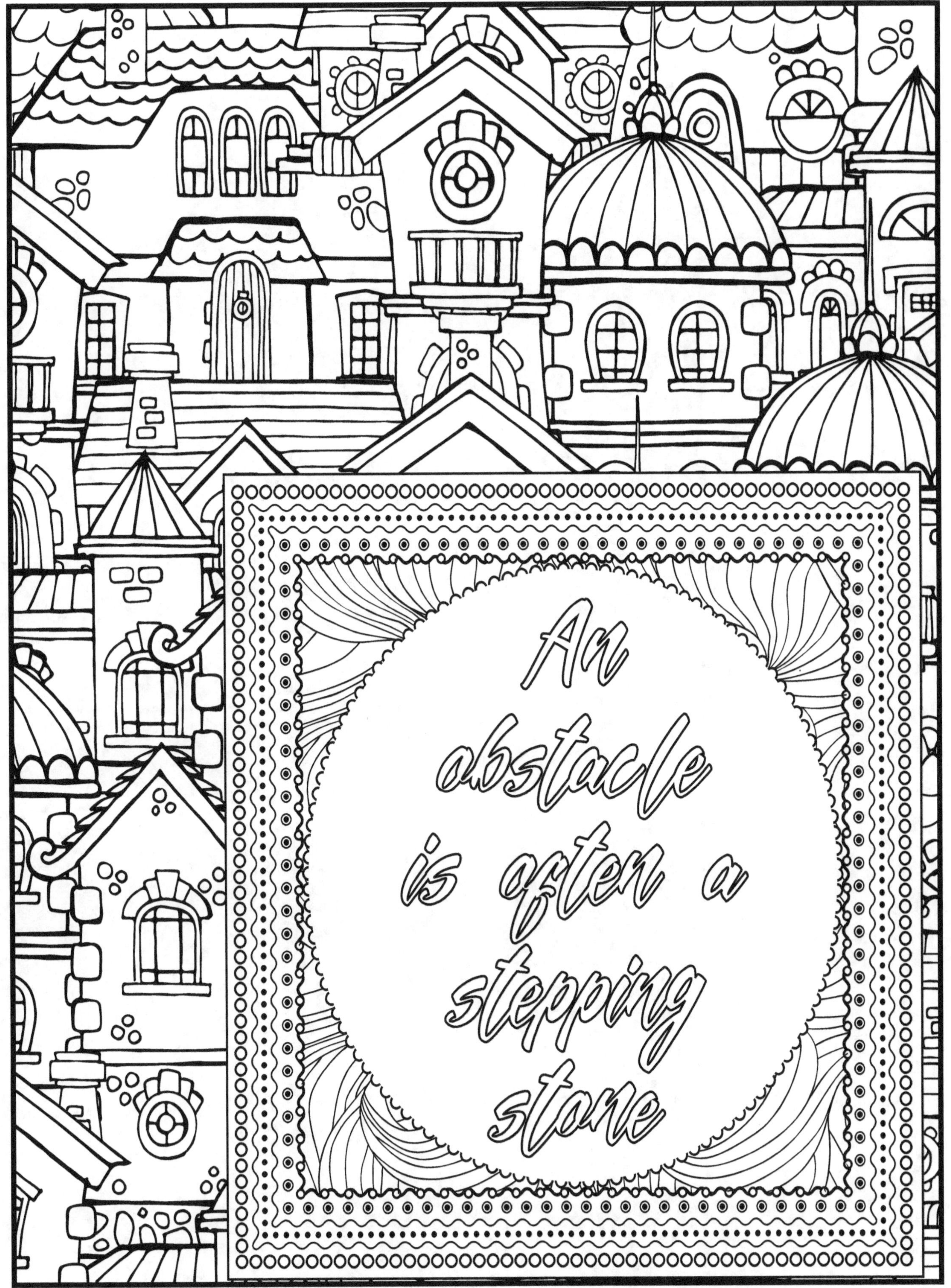
An obstacle is often a stepping stone

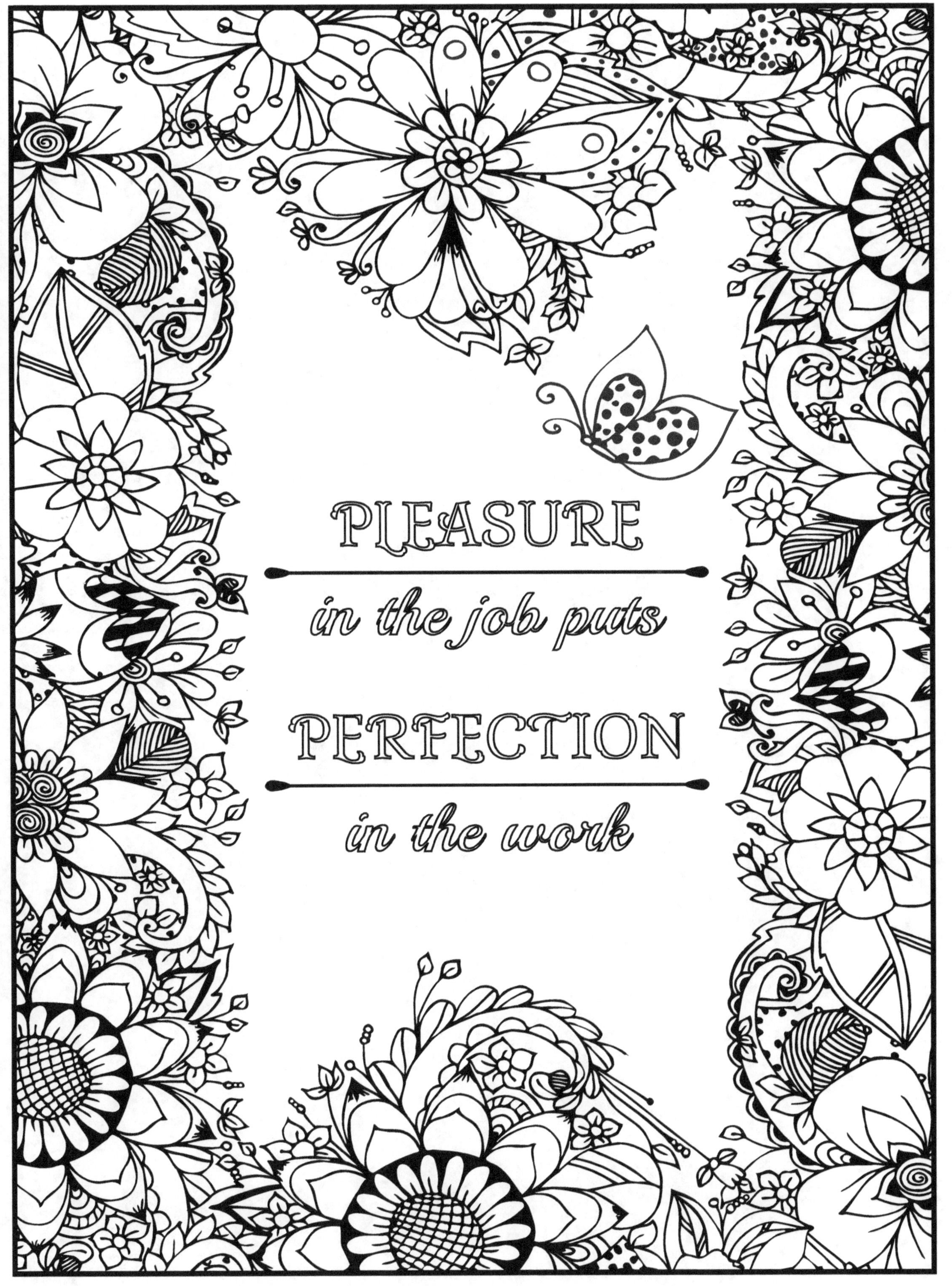

PLEASURE
in the job puts
PERFECTION
in the work

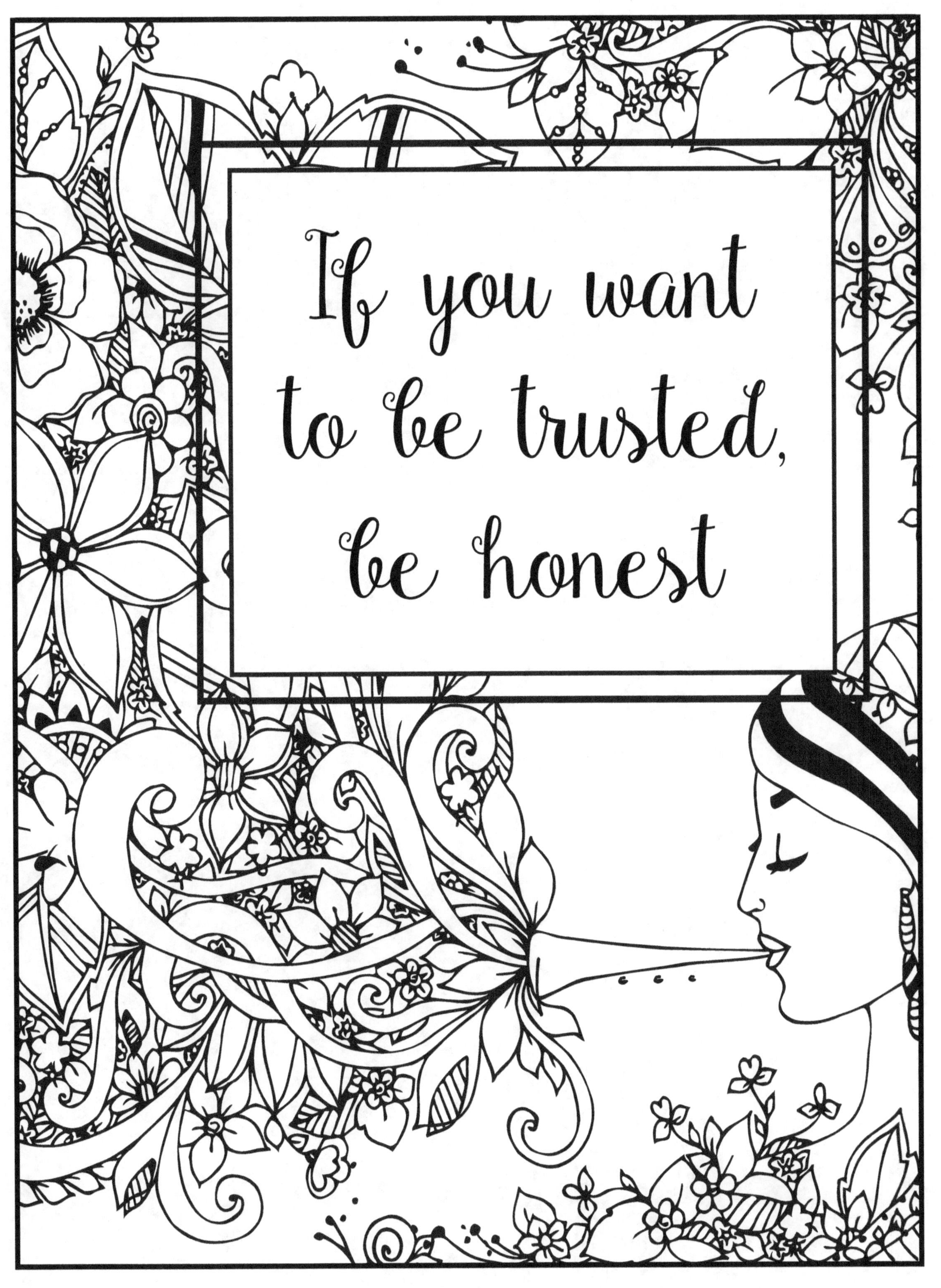

If you want
to be trusted,
be honest

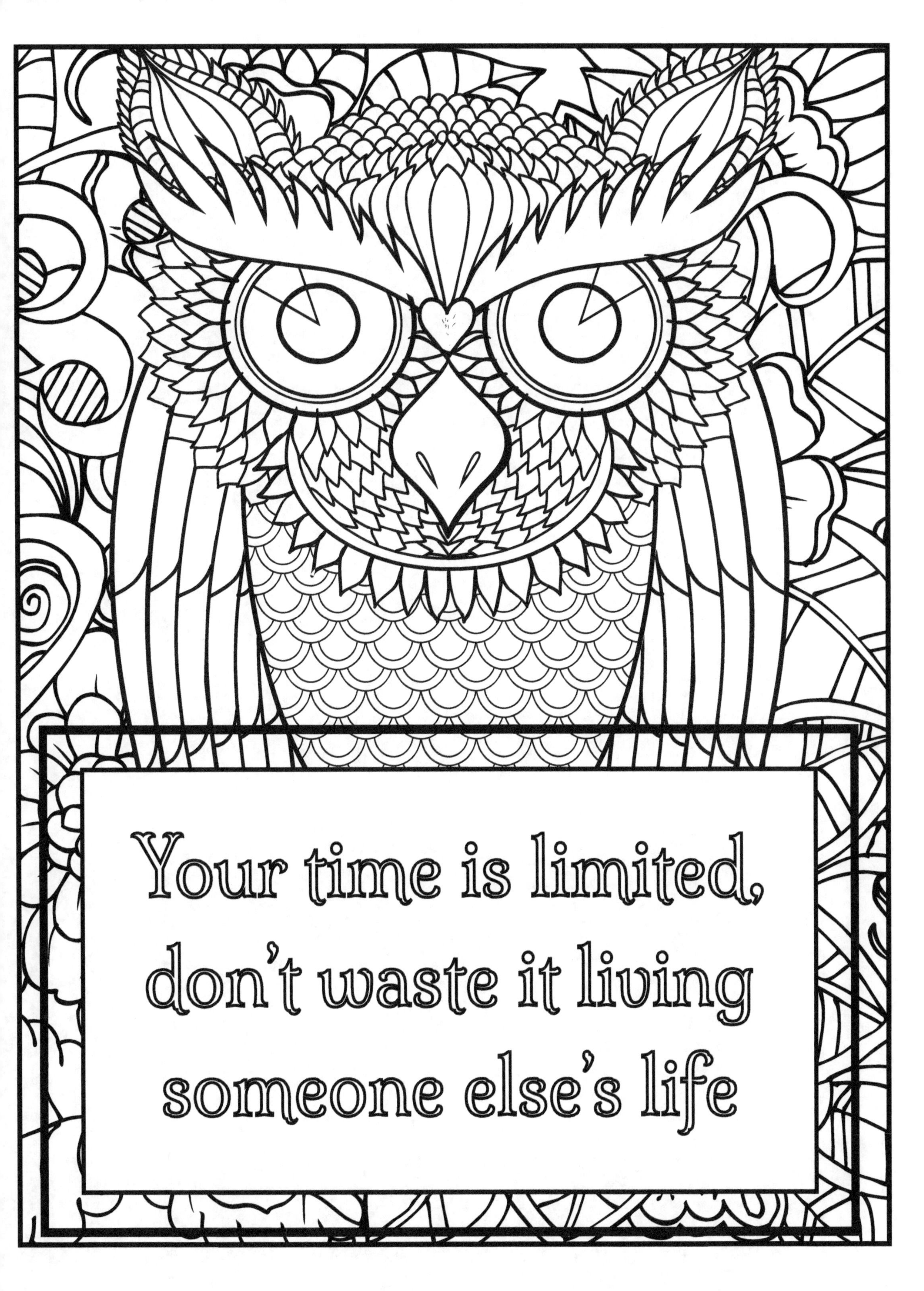

Your time is limited,
don't waste it living
someone else's life

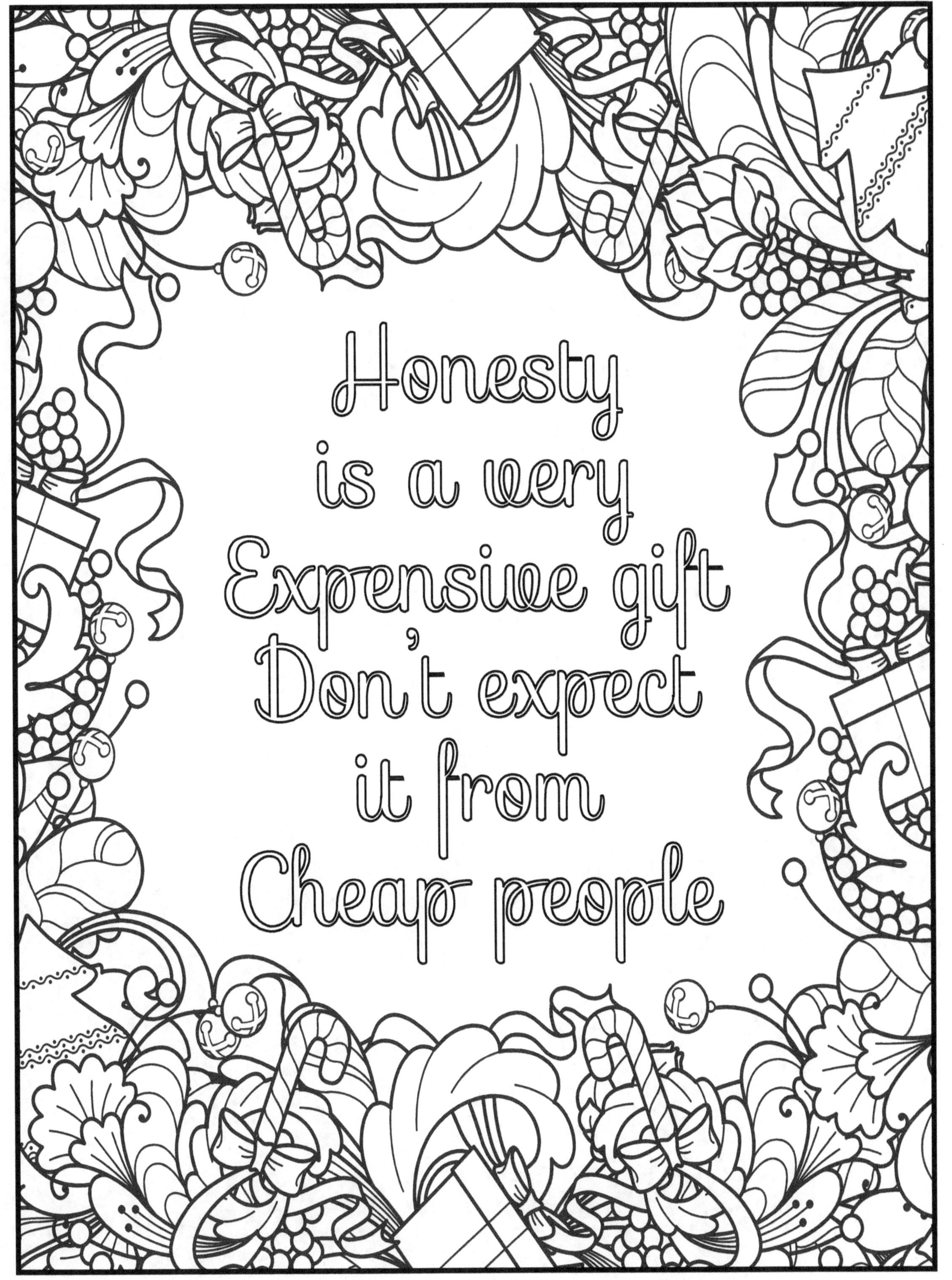

Honesty
is a very
Expensive gift,
Don't expect
it from
Cheap people

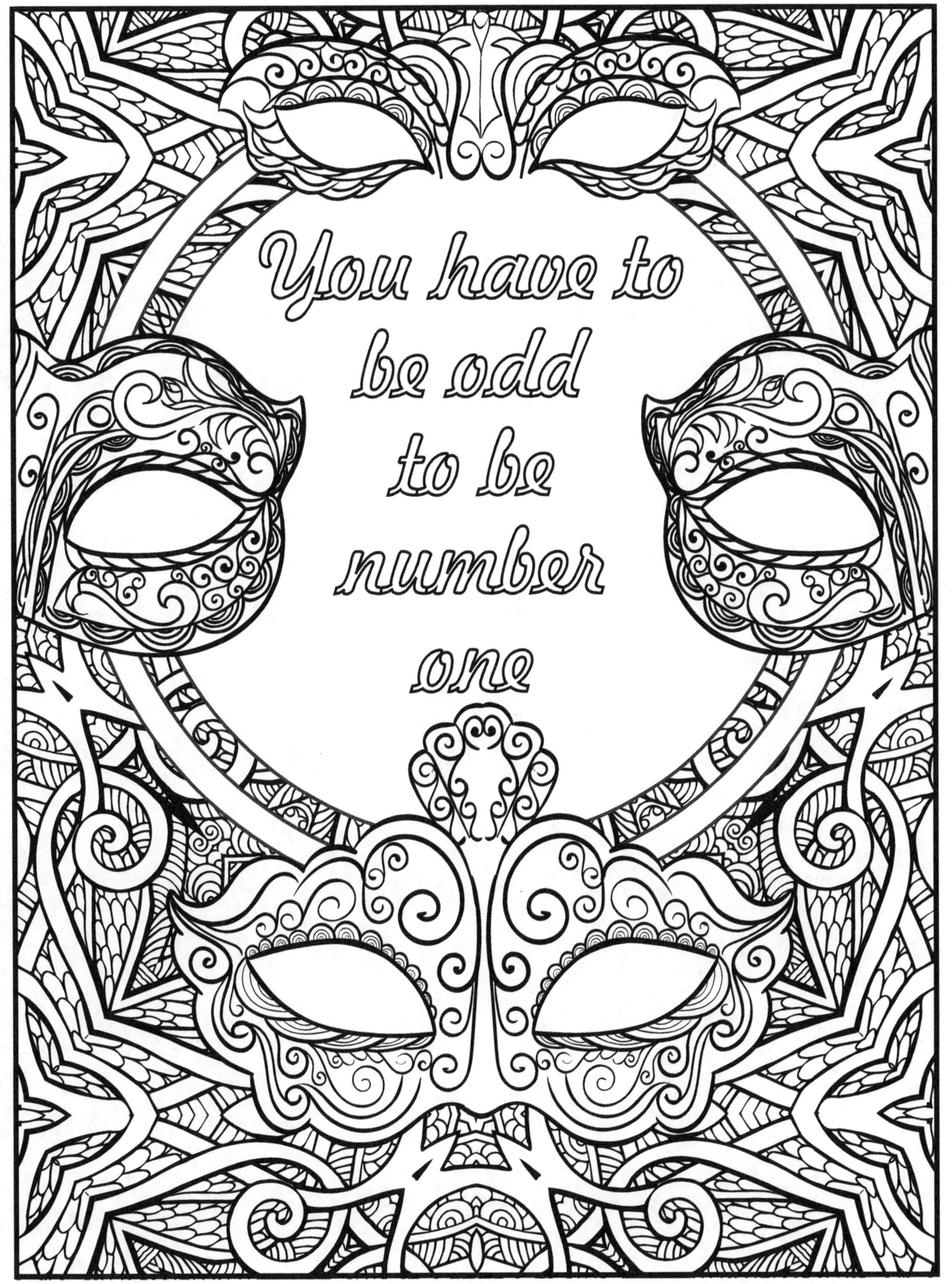

You have to
be odd
to be
number
one

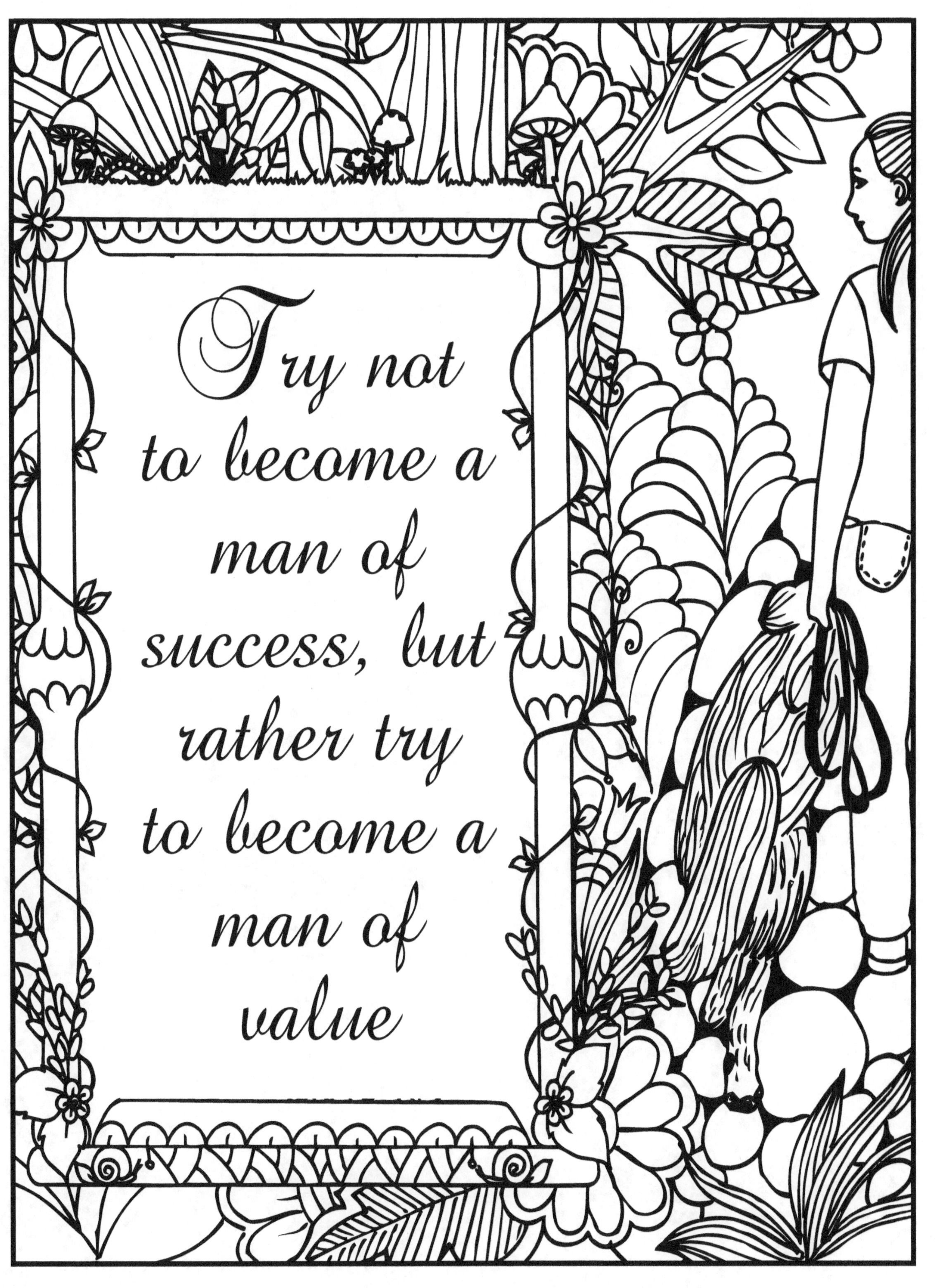

Try not
to become a
man of
success, but
rather try
to become a
man of
value

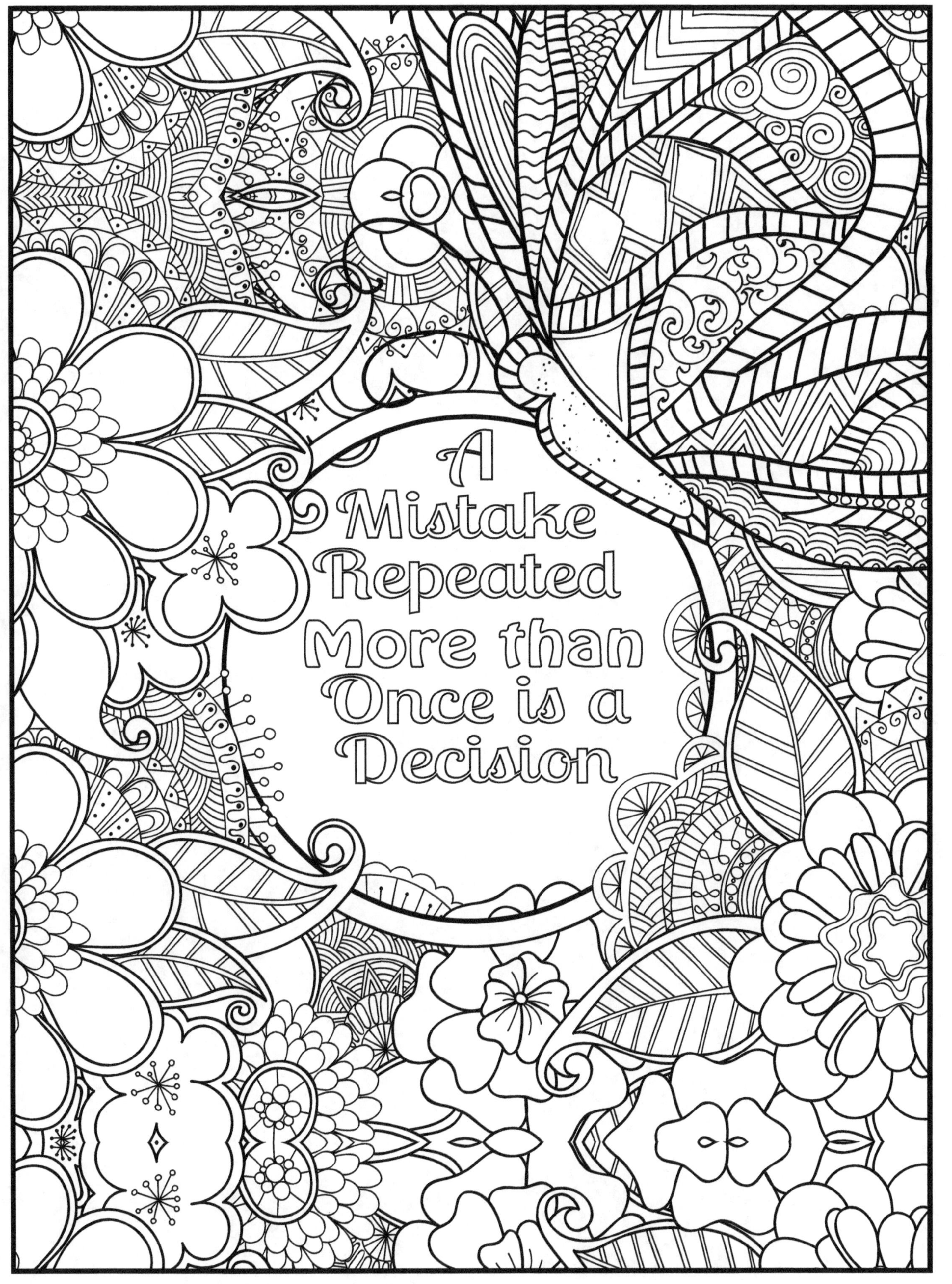

A
Mistake
Repeated
More than
Once is a
Decision

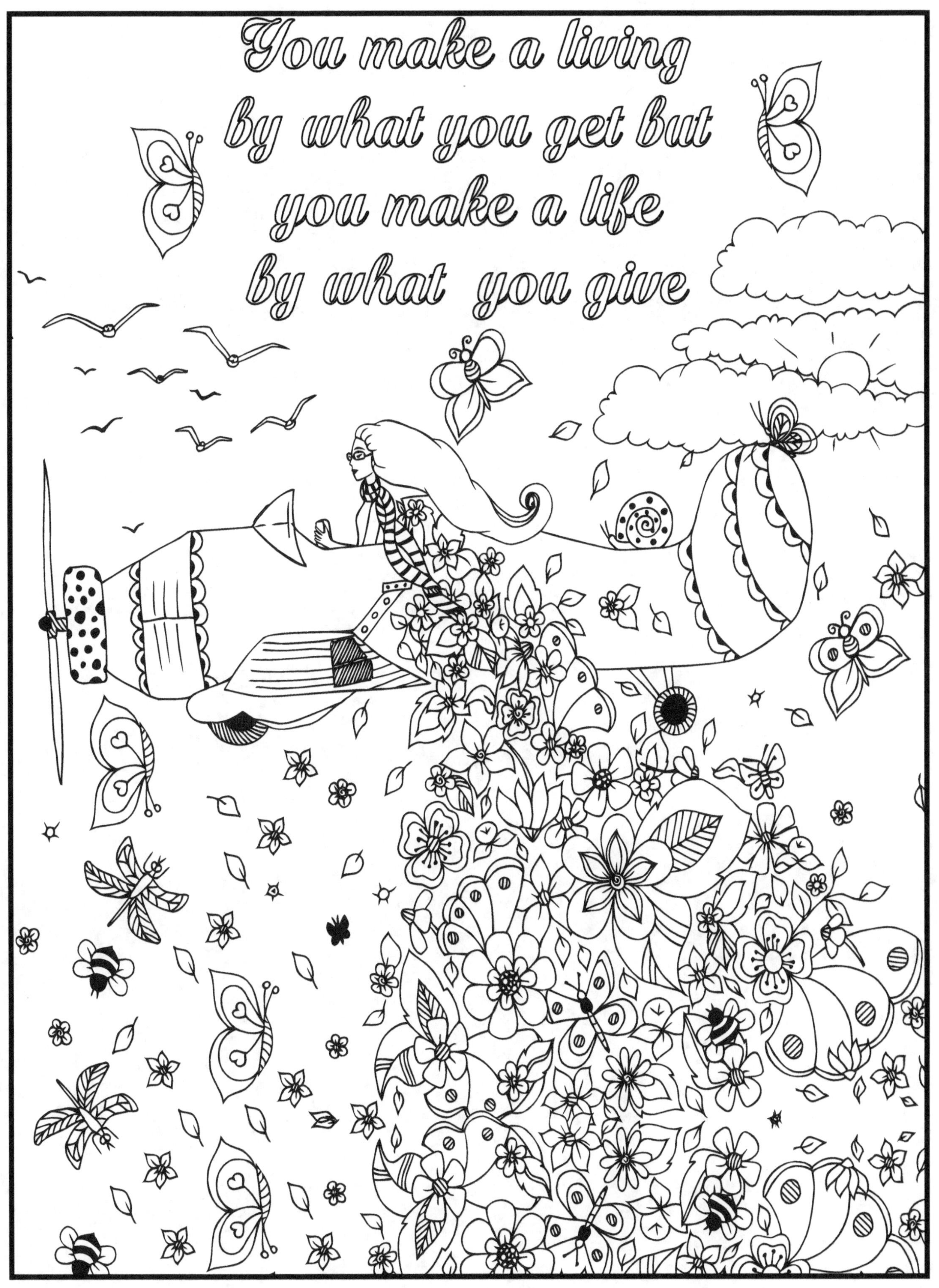

You make a living
by what you get but
you make a life
by what you give

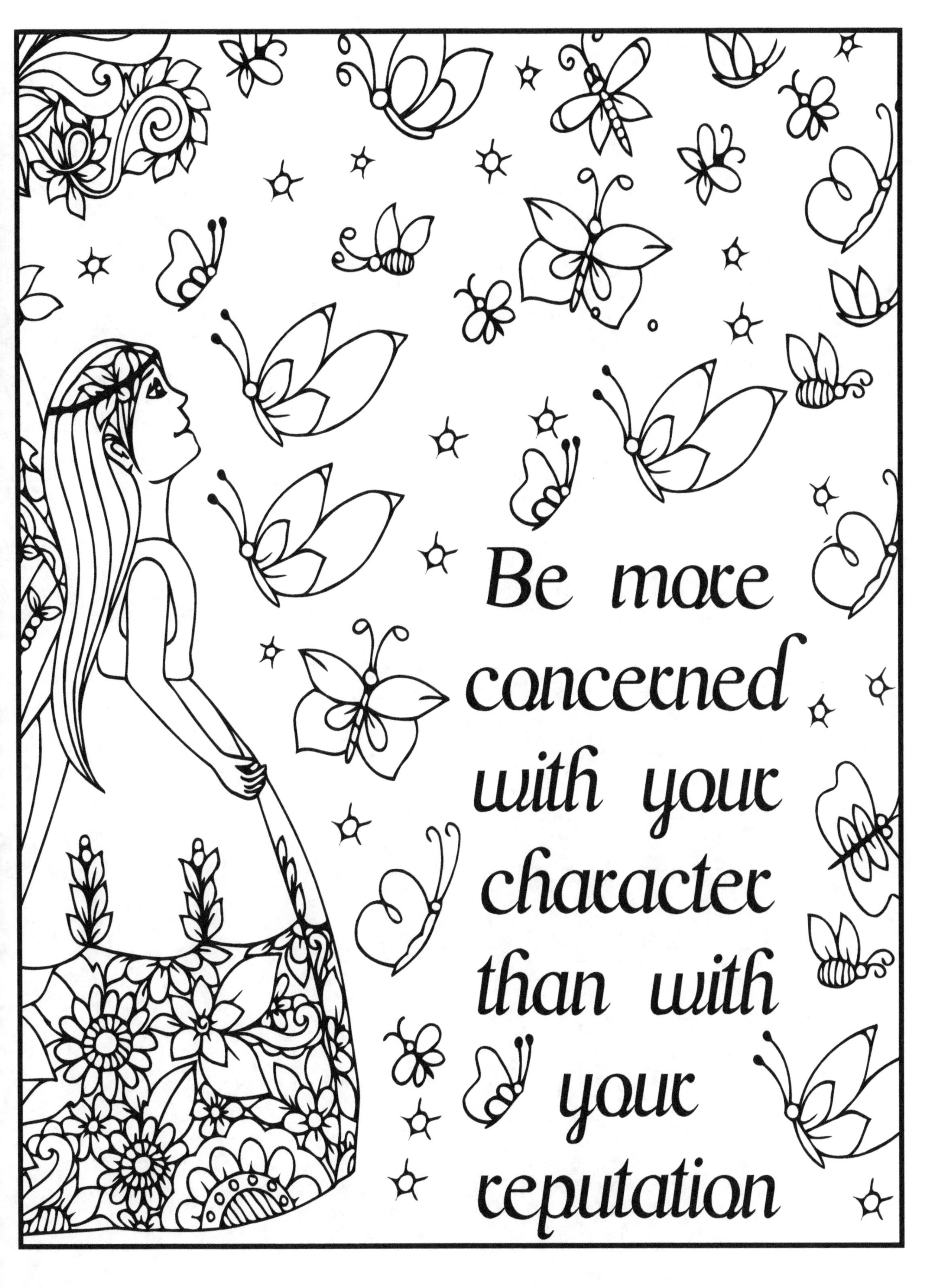
Be more concerned with your character than with your reputation

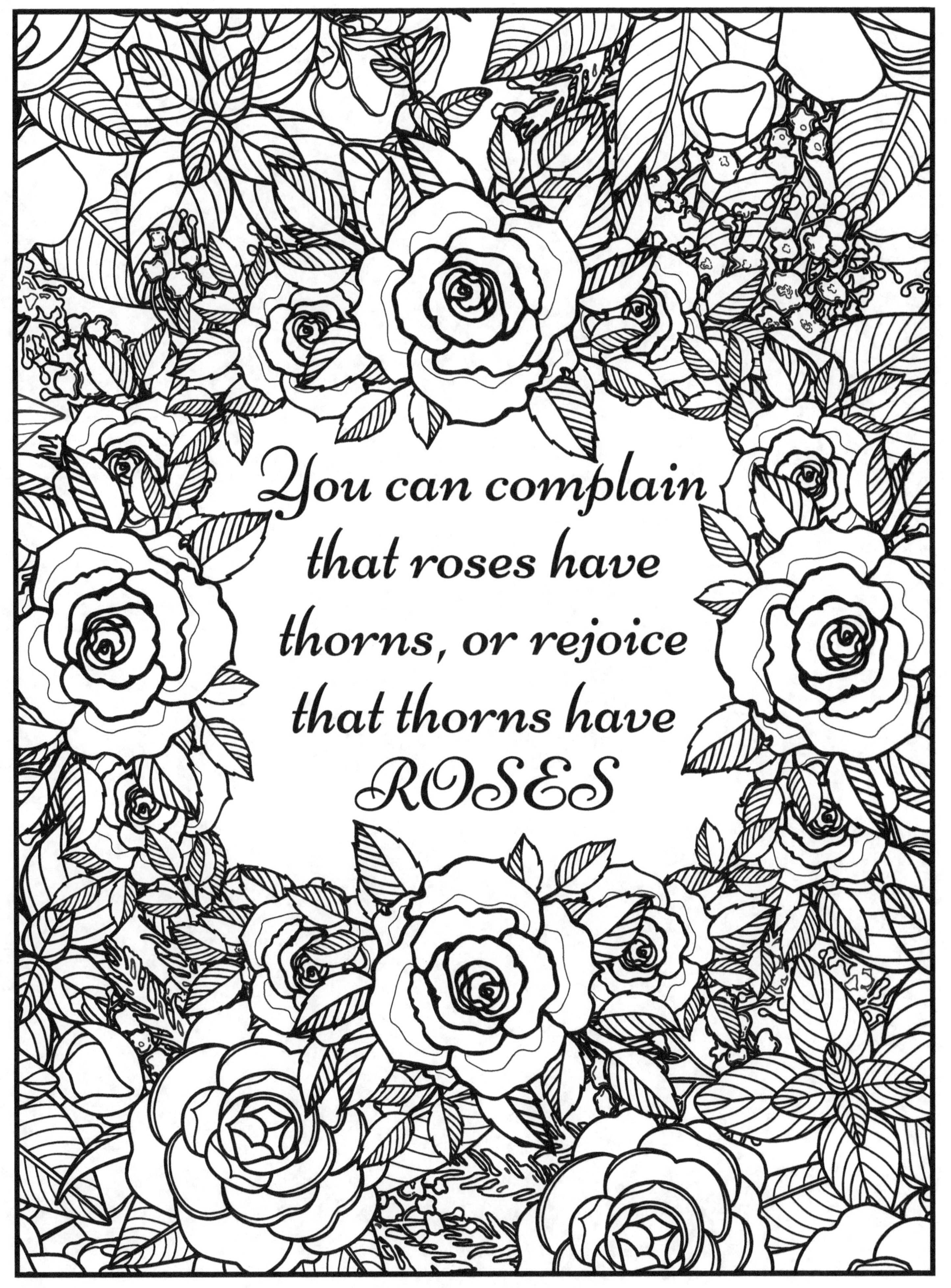

You can complain
that roses have
thorns, or rejoice
that thorns have
ROSES

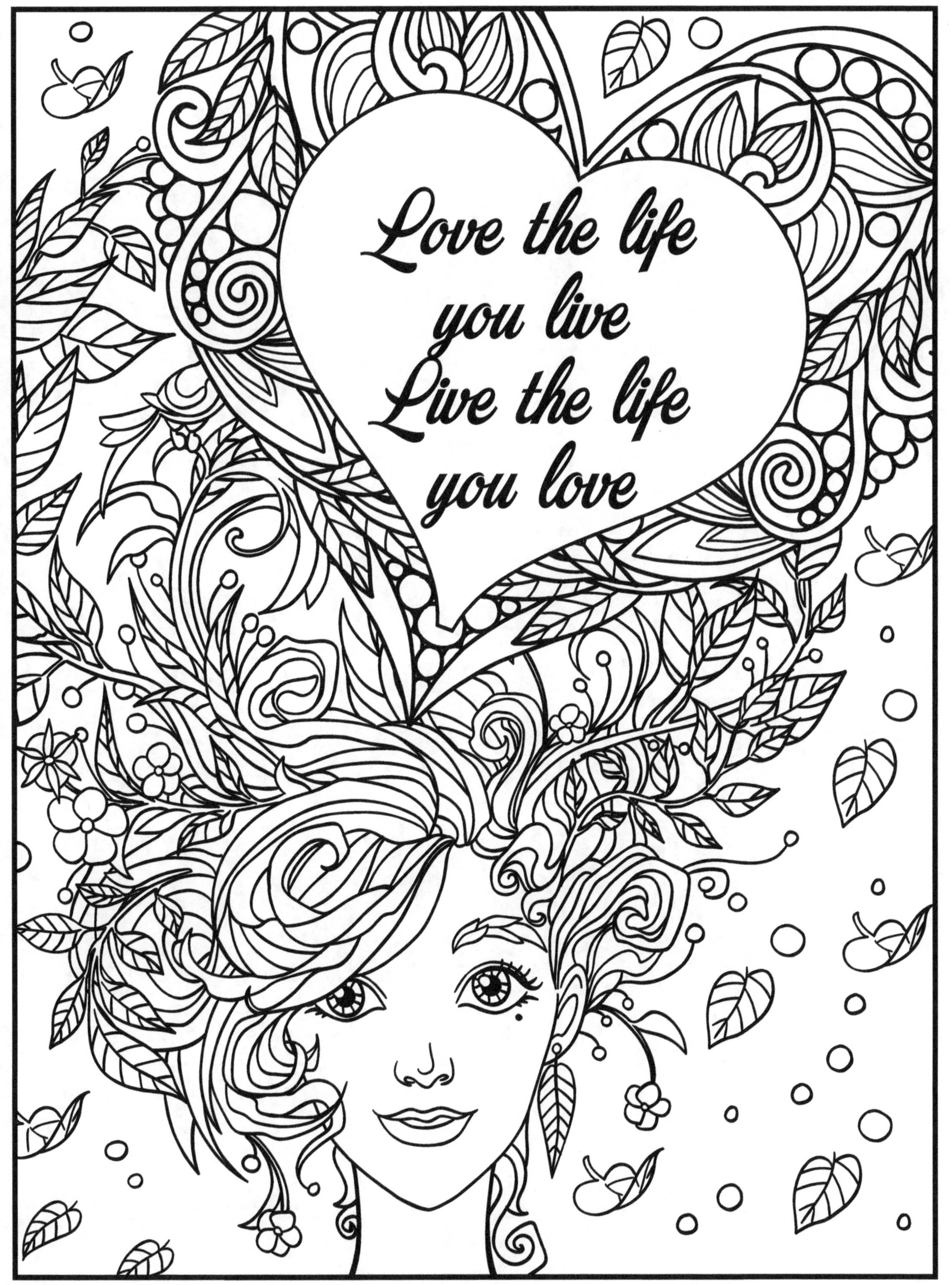

Love the life
you live
Live the life
you love

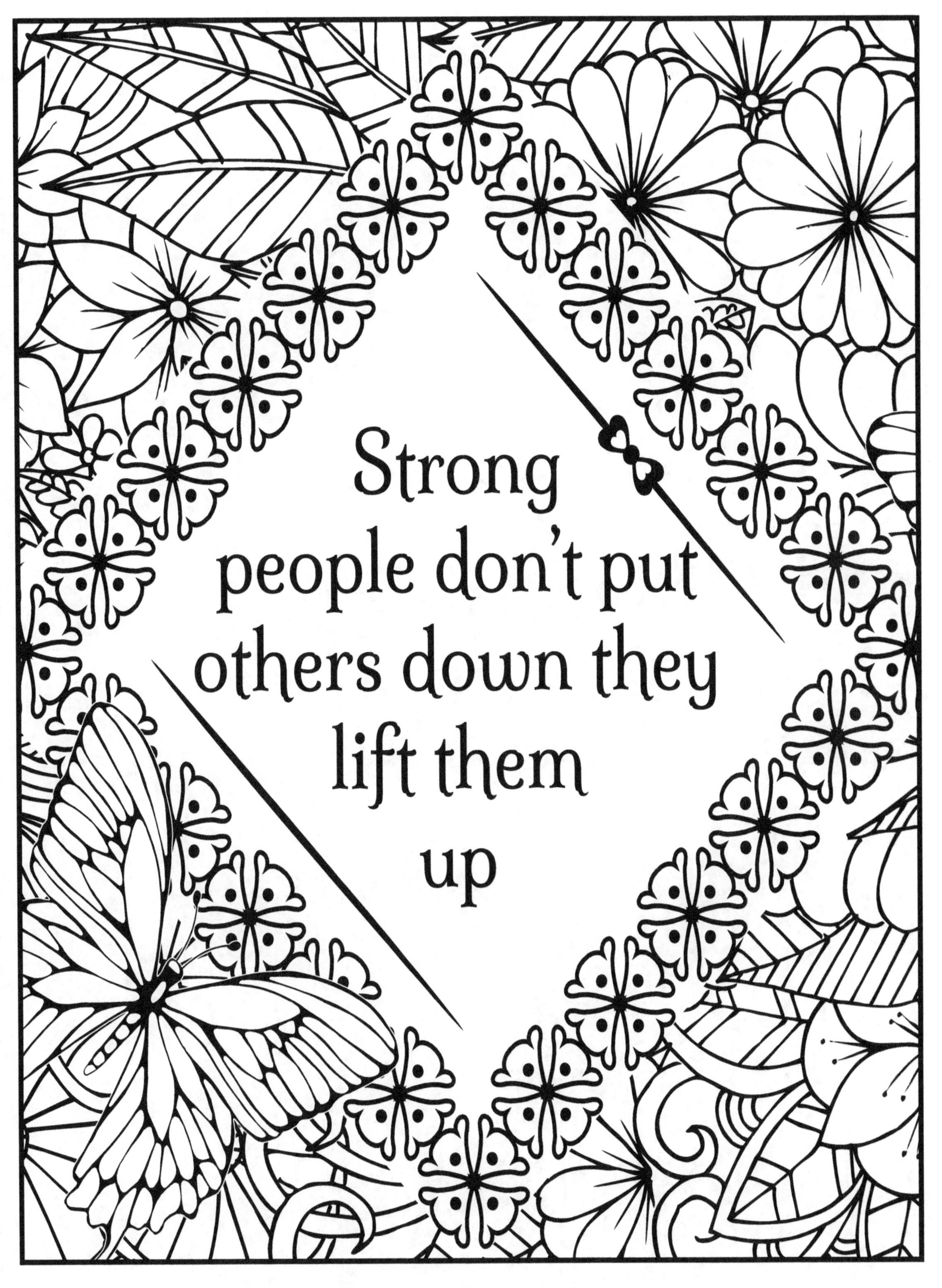
Strong
people don't put
others down they
lift them
up

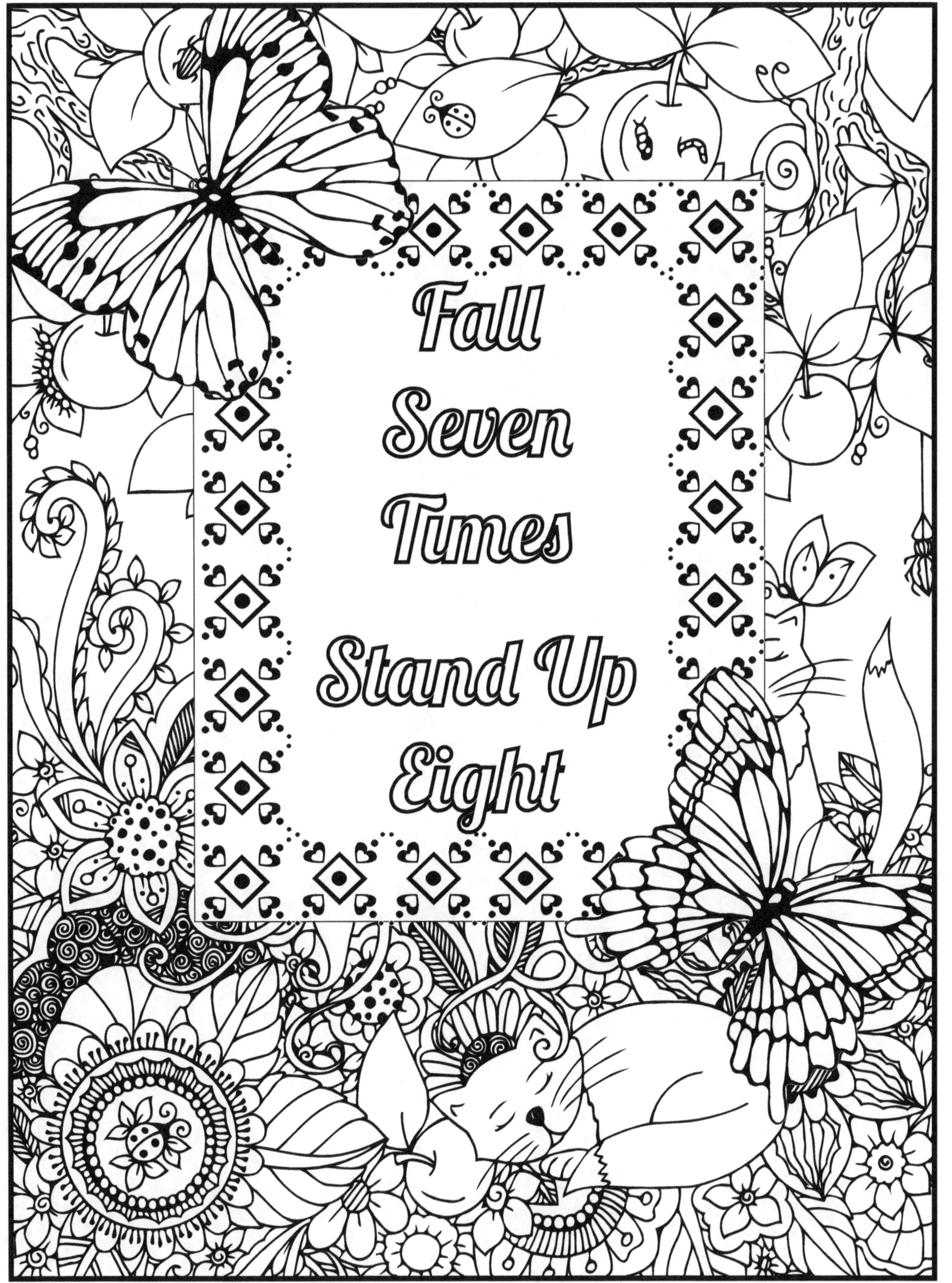

Fall
Seven
Times
Stand Up
Eight

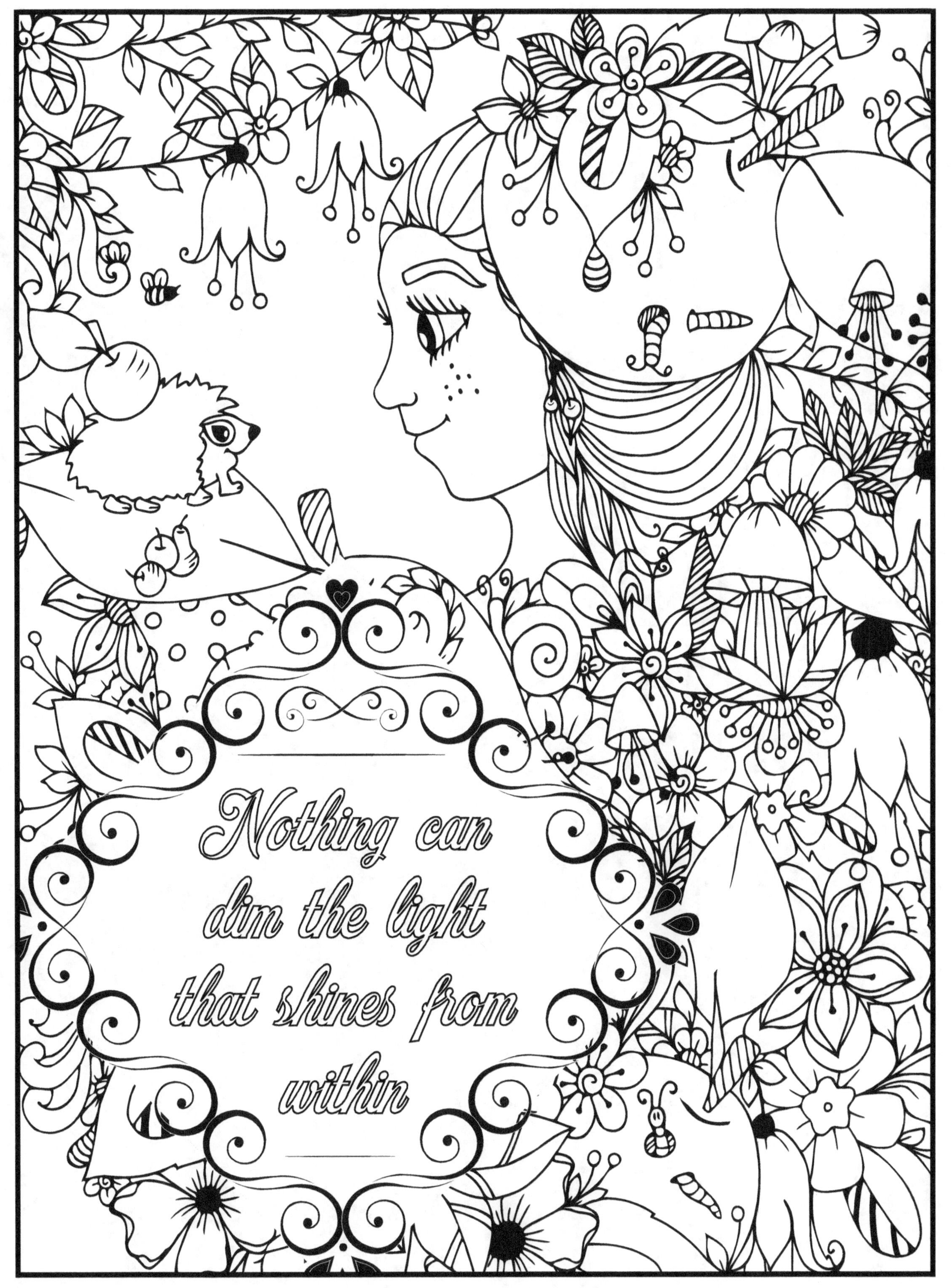

Nothing can
dim the light
that shines from
within

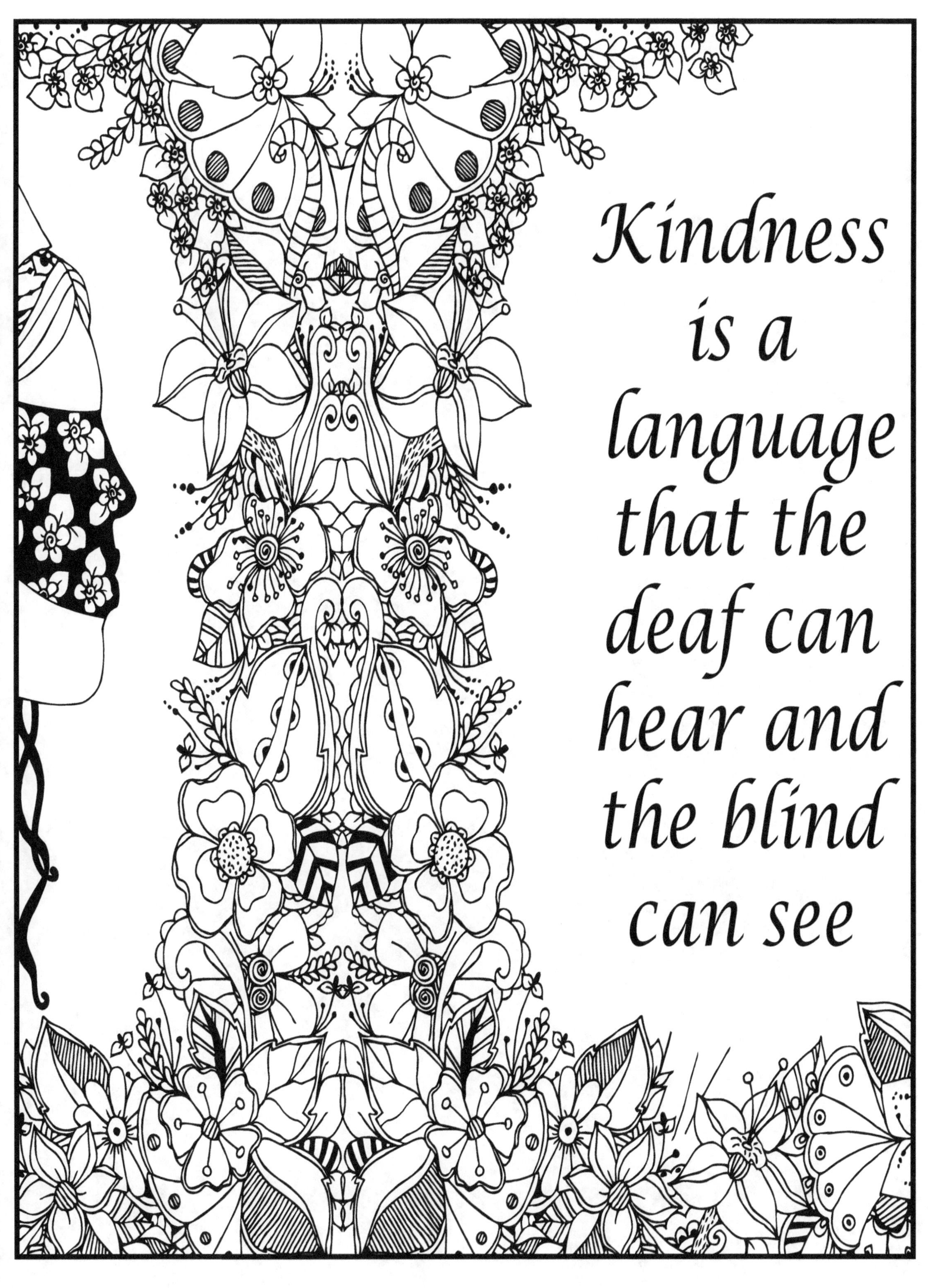

Kindness
is a
language
that the
deaf can
hear and
the blind
can see

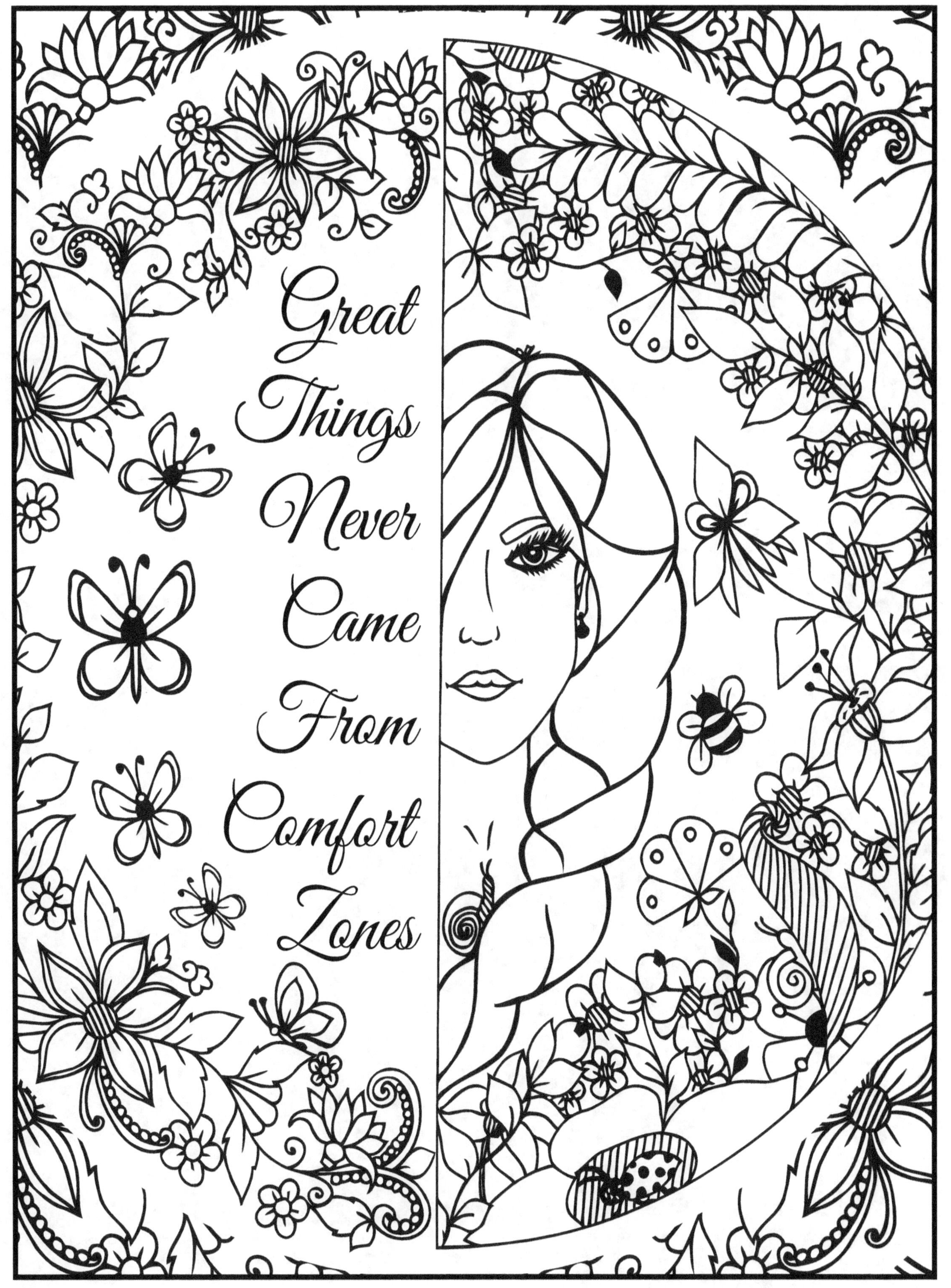

Great
Things
Never
Came
From
Comfort
Zones

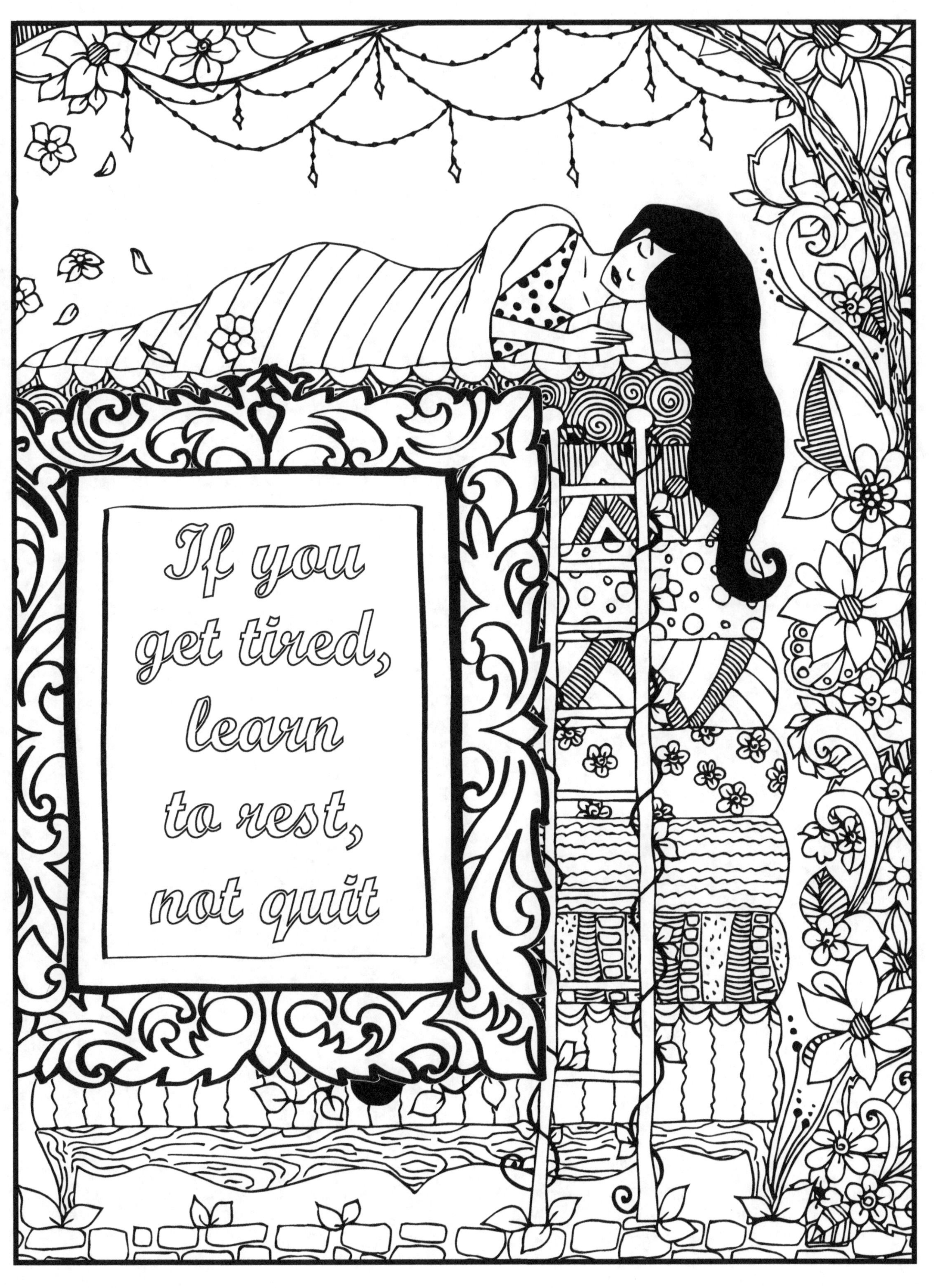

If you
get tired,
learn
to rest,
not quit

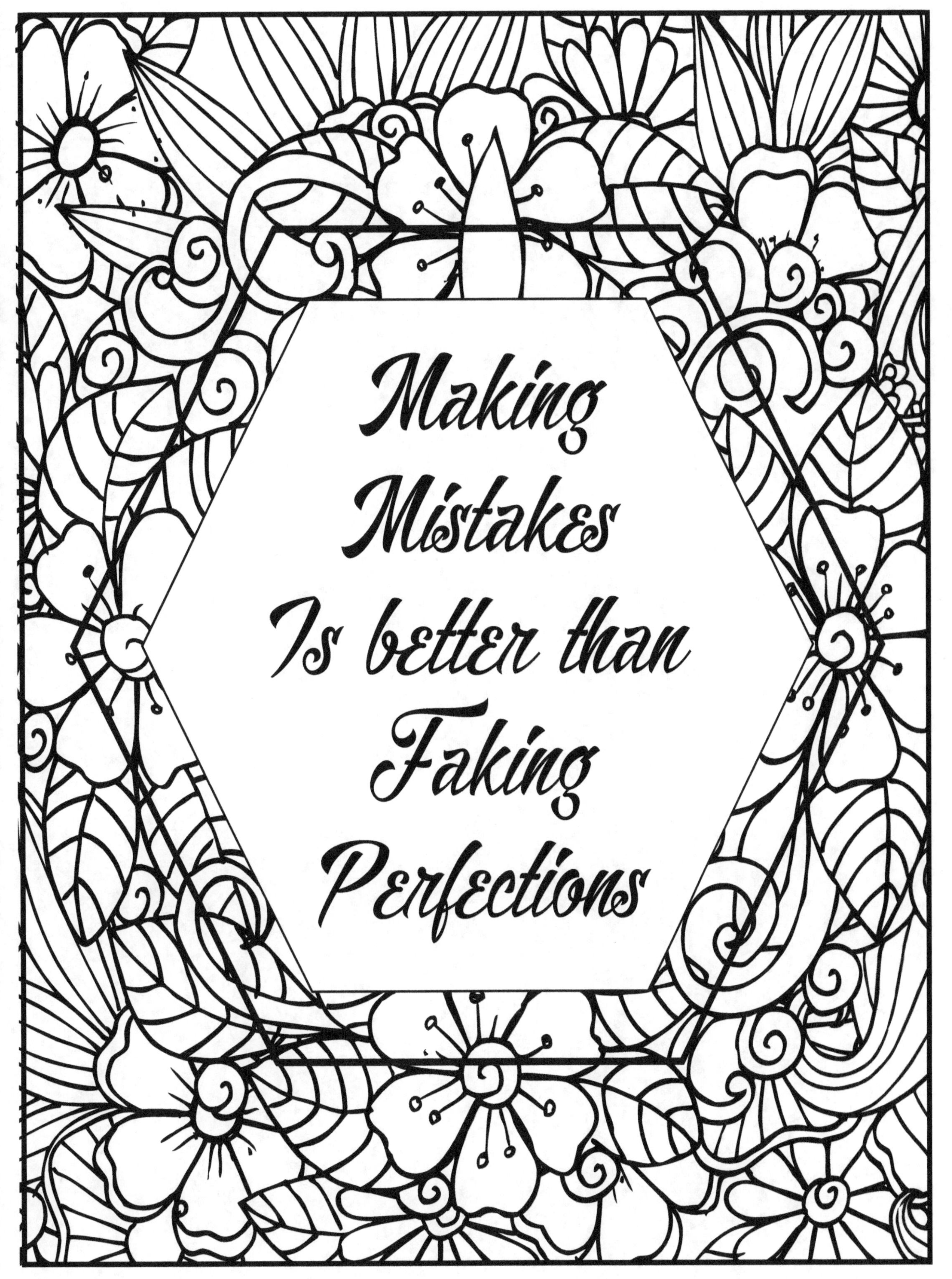

Making
Mistakes
Is better than
Faking
Perfections

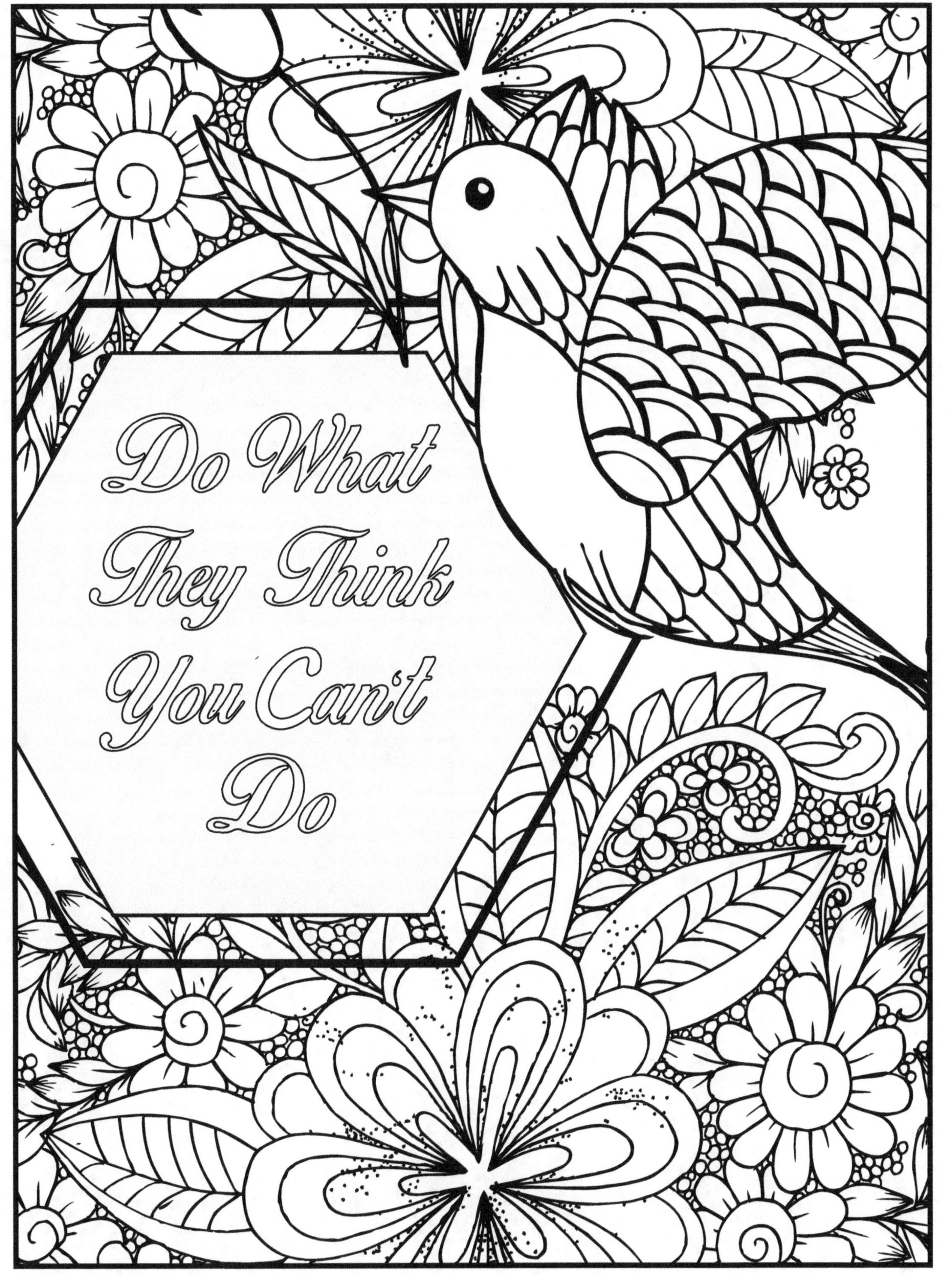
Do What
They Think
You Can't
Do

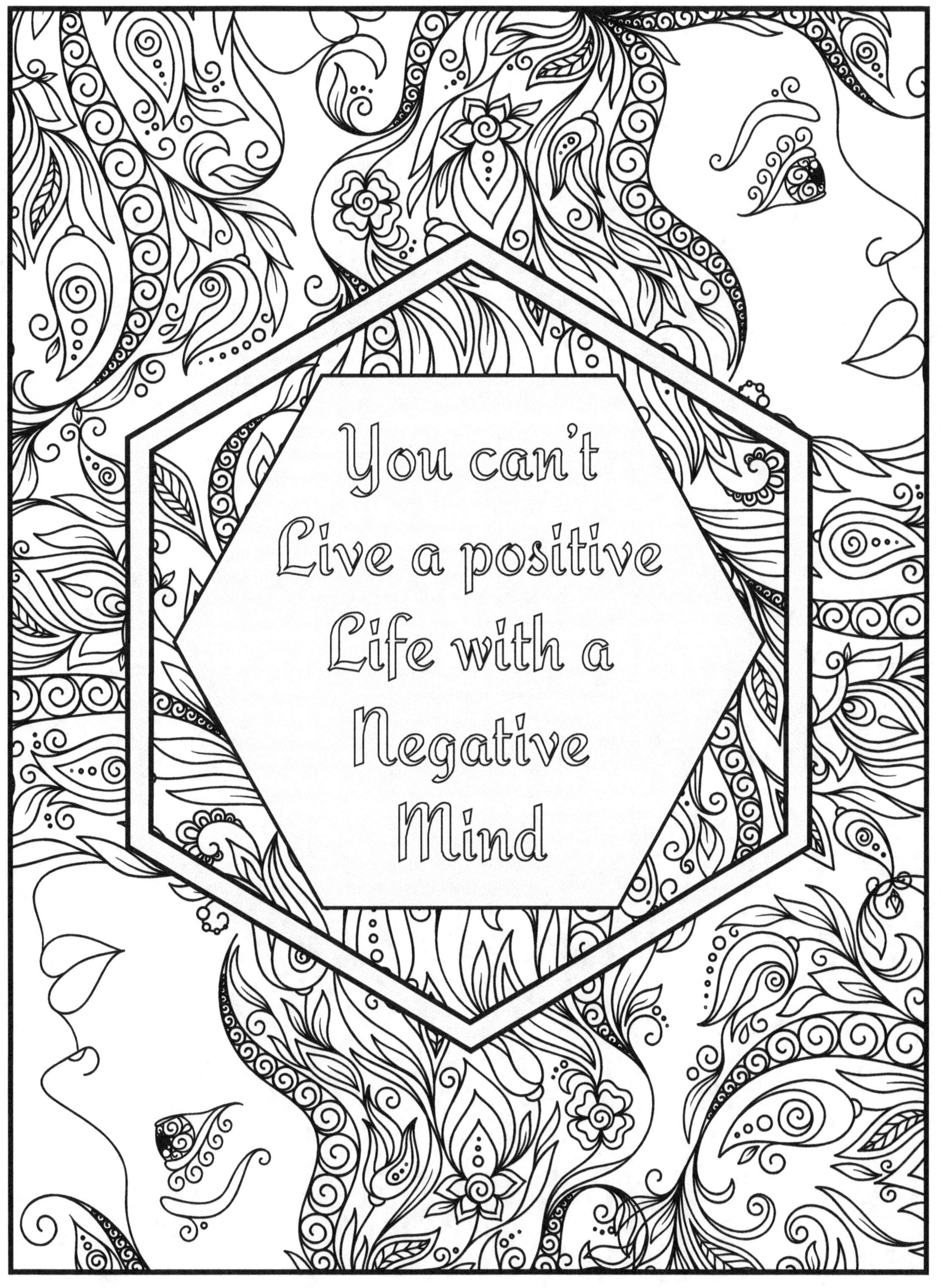

You can't
Live a positive
Life with a
Negative
Mind

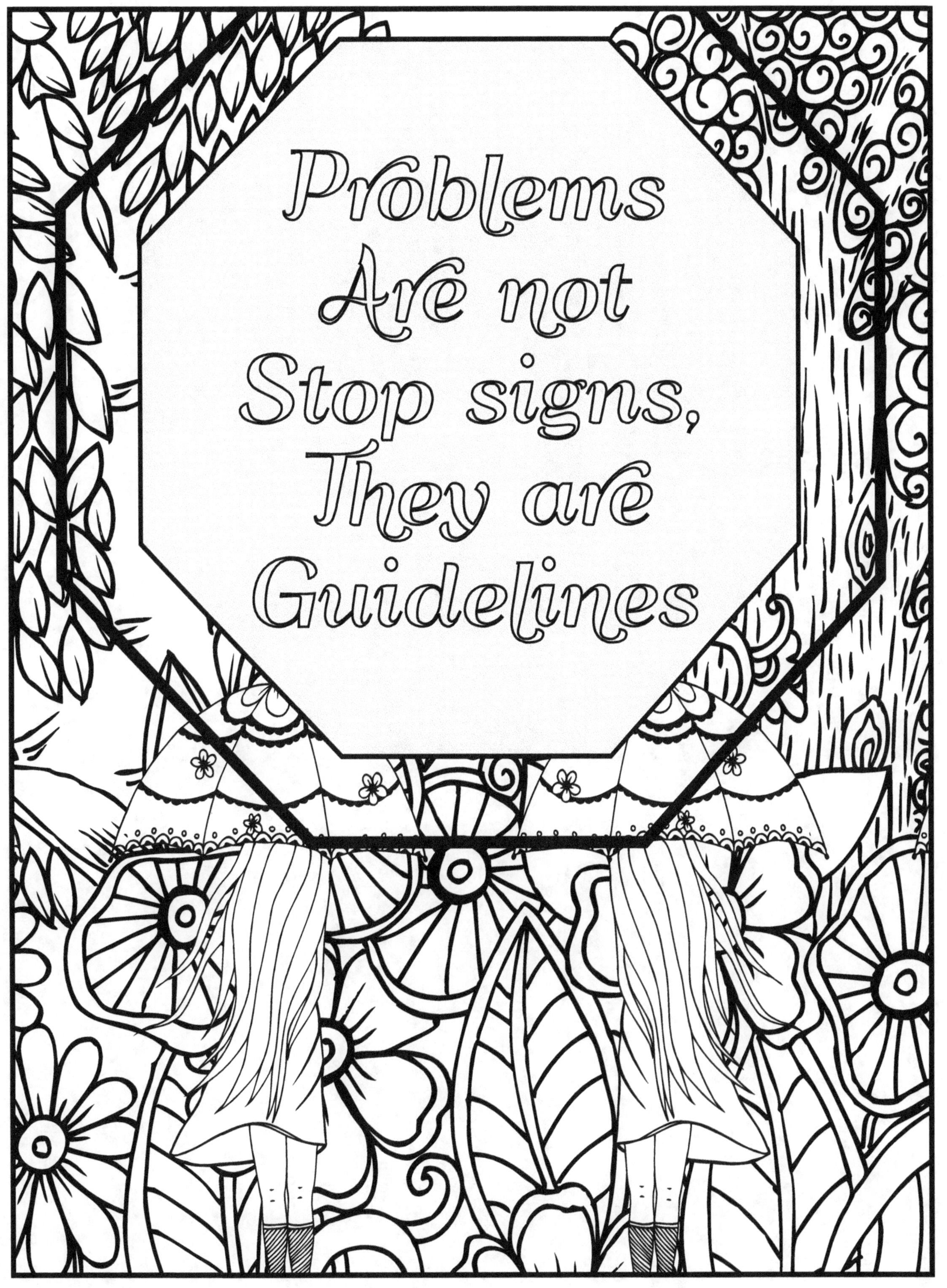

Problems
Are not
Stop signs,
They are
Guidelines

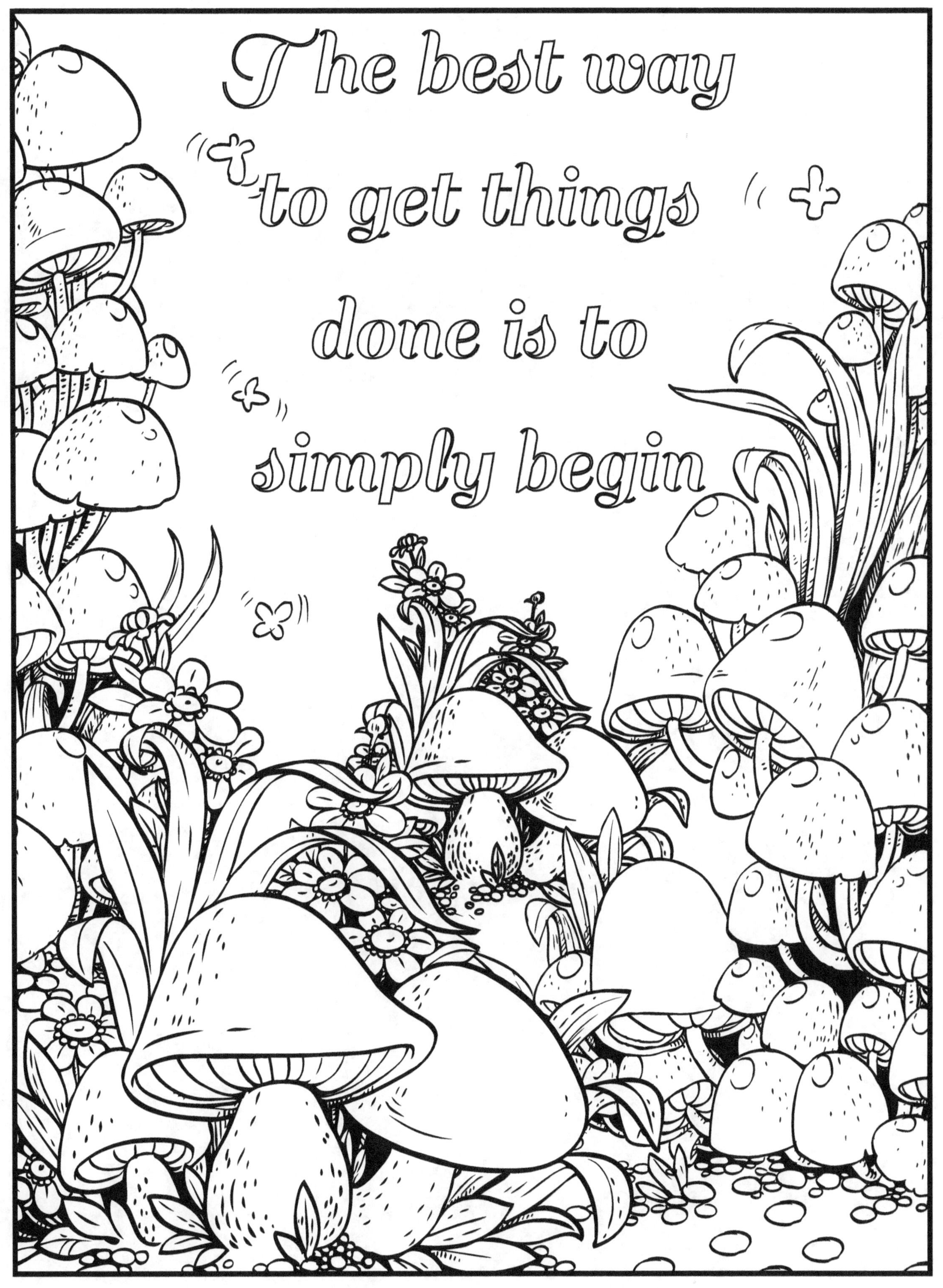
The best way
to get things
done is to
simply begin

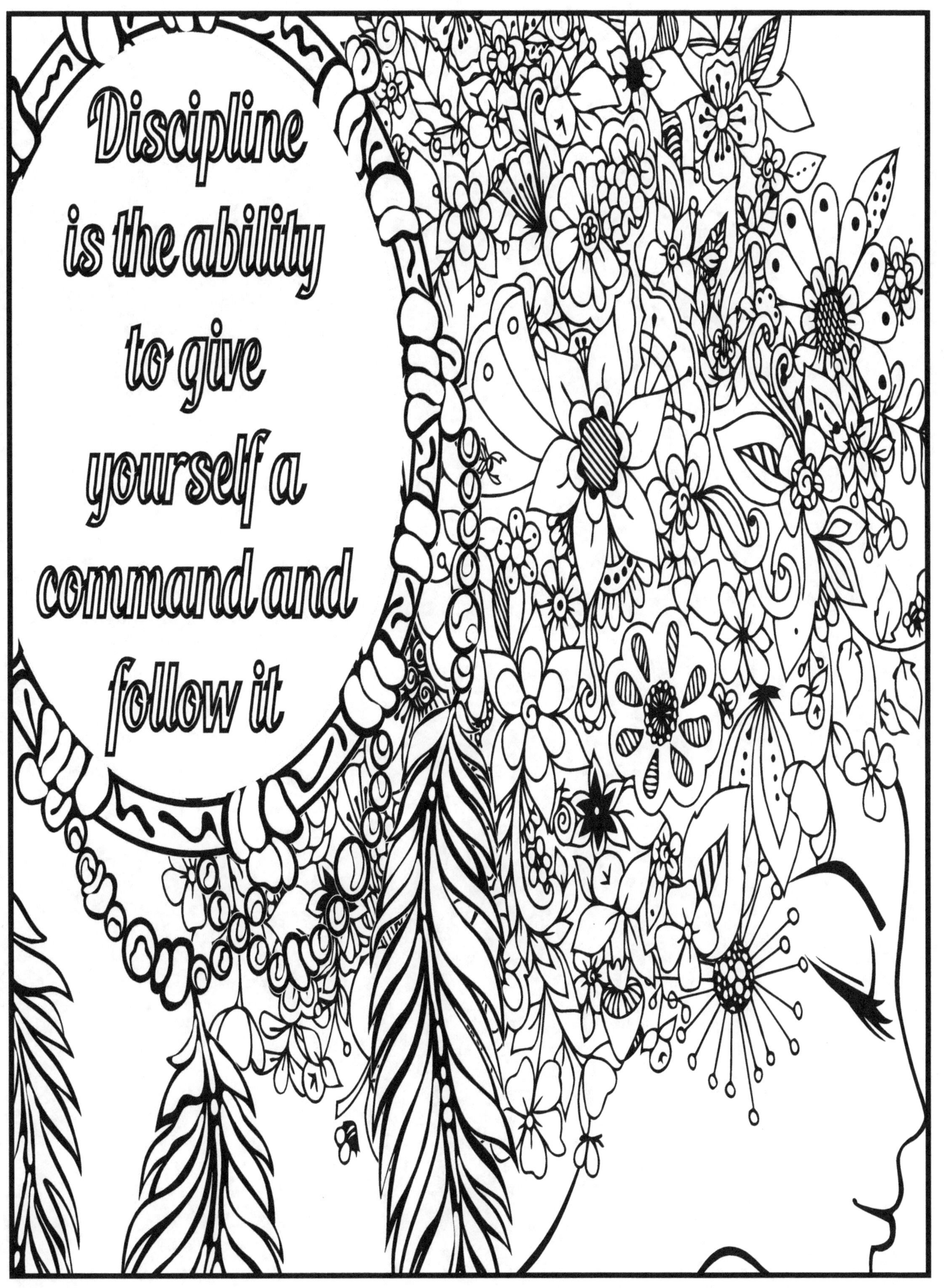

Discipline
is the ability
to give
yourself a
command and
follow it

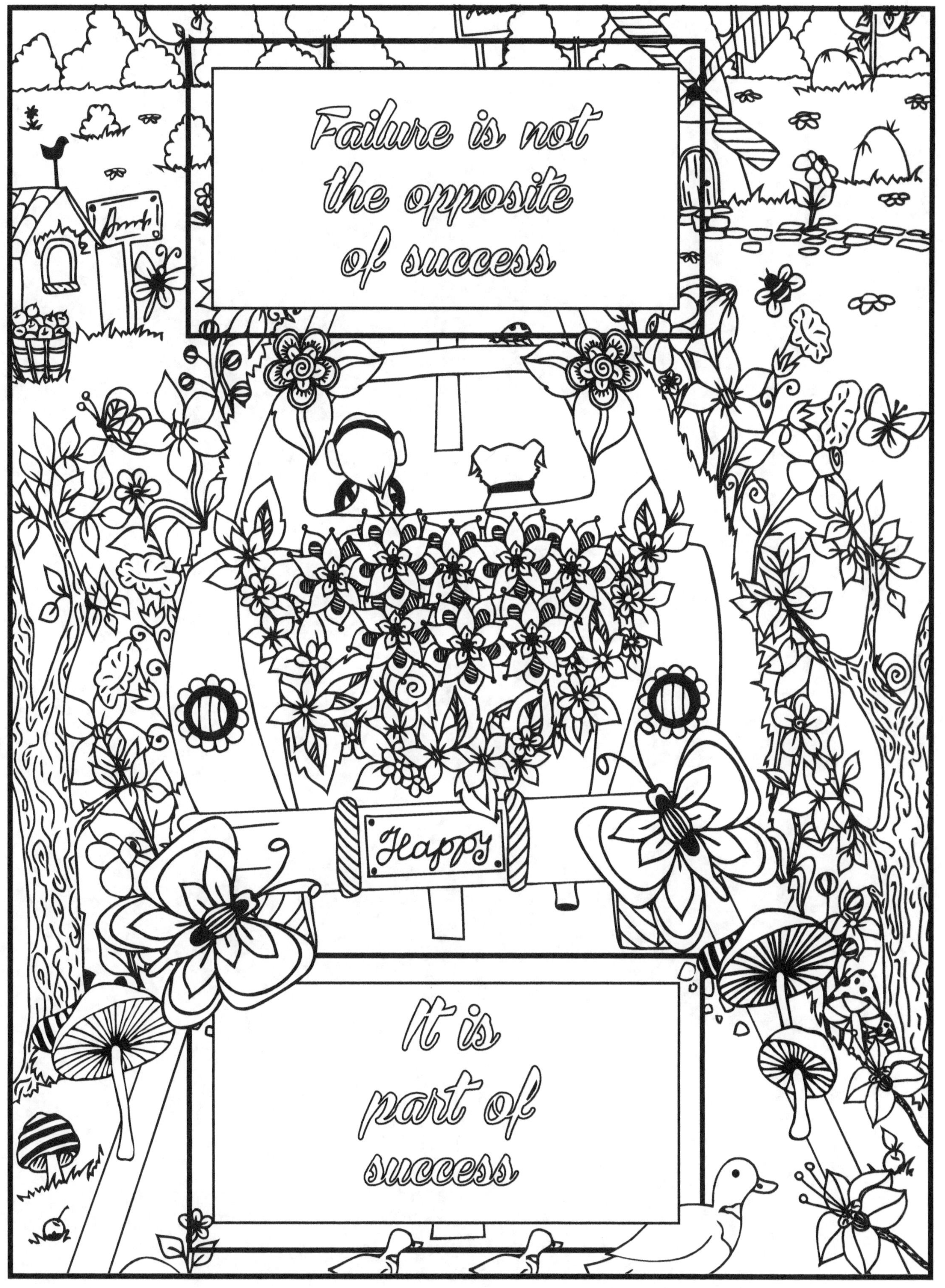

Failure is not
the opposite
of success

Happy

It is
part of
success

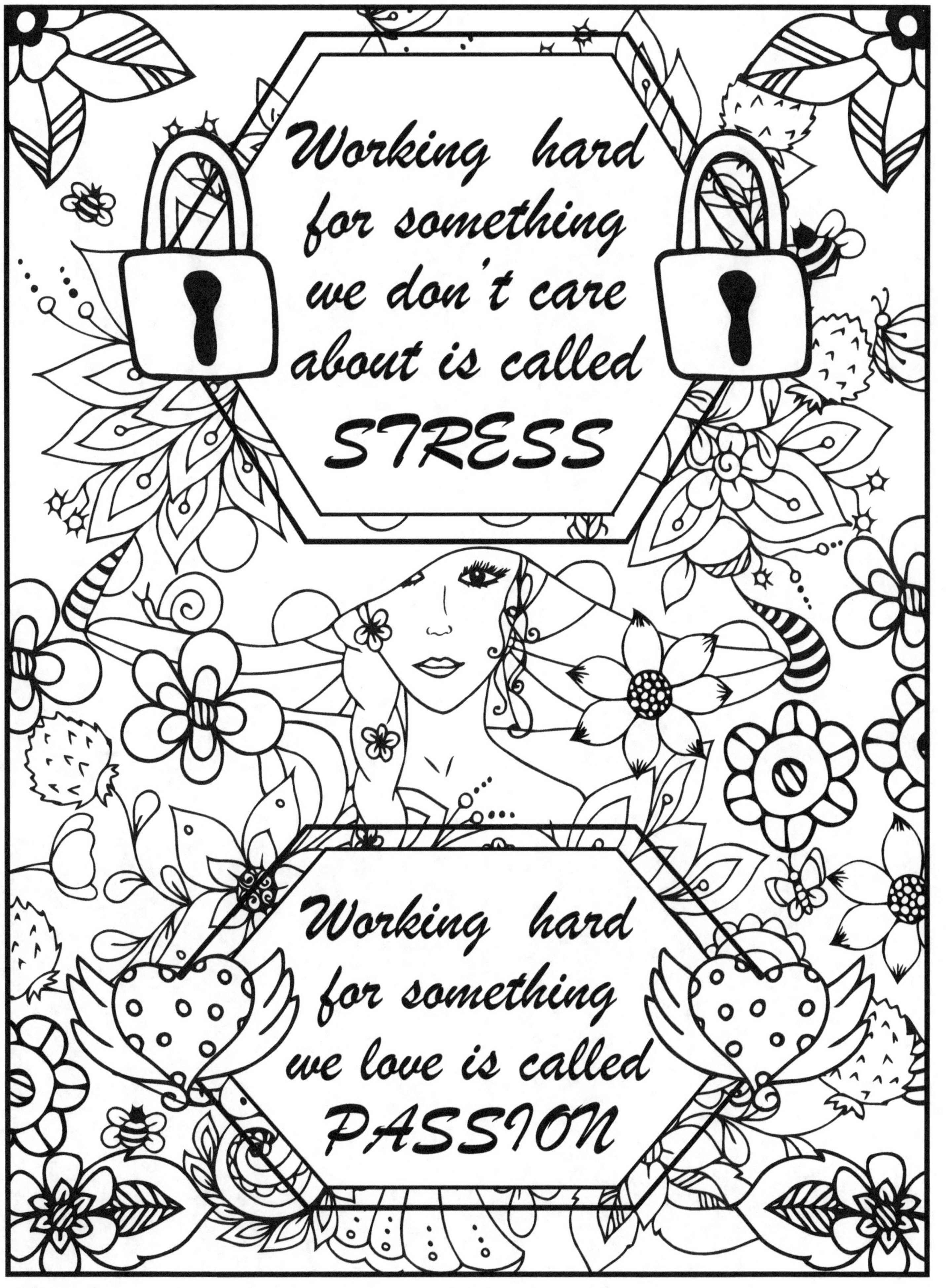

Working hard
for something
we don't care
about is called
STRESS
Working hard
for something
we love is called
PASSION

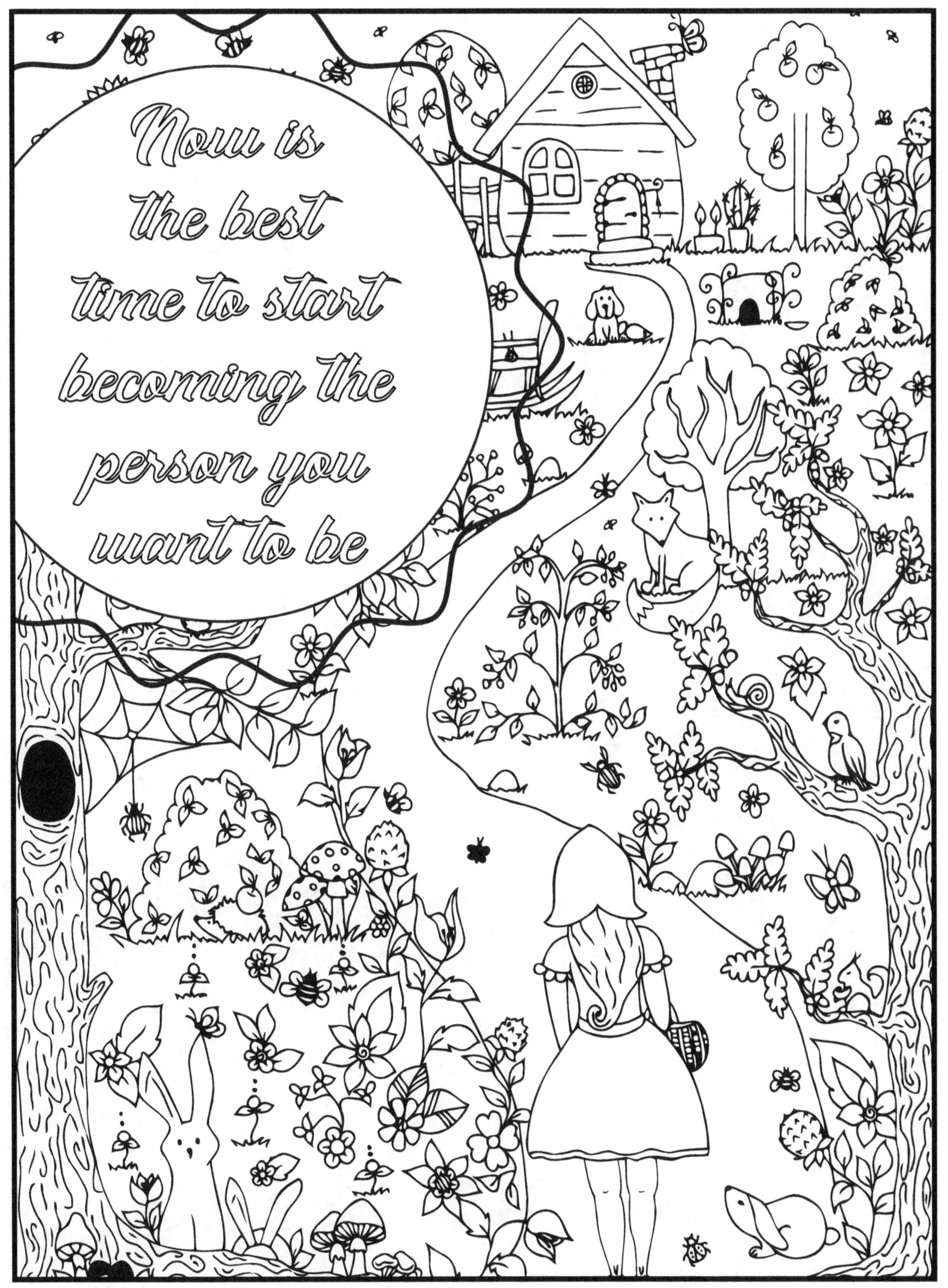

Now is
the best
time to start
becoming the
person you
want to be

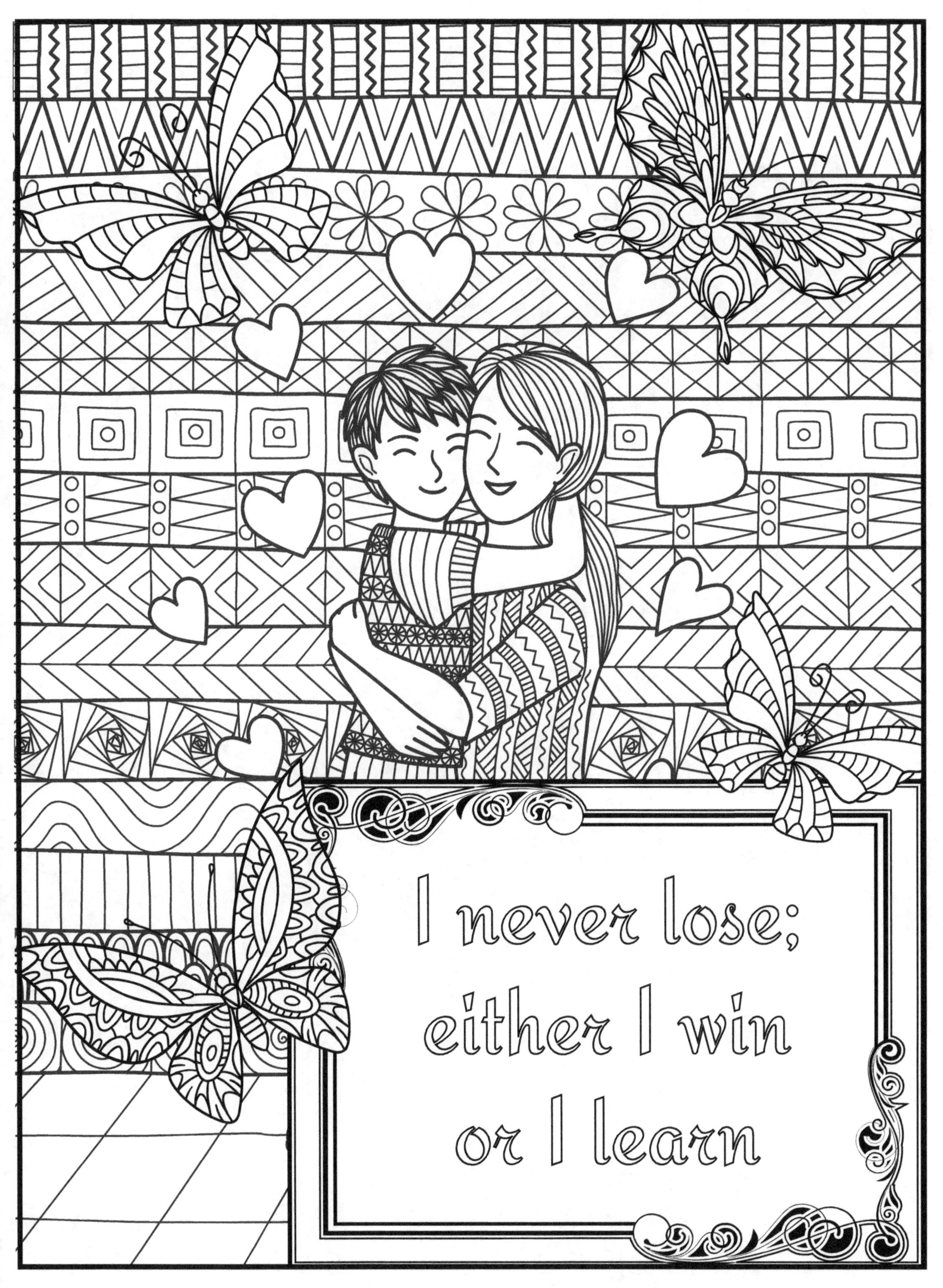

I never lose;
either I win
or I learn

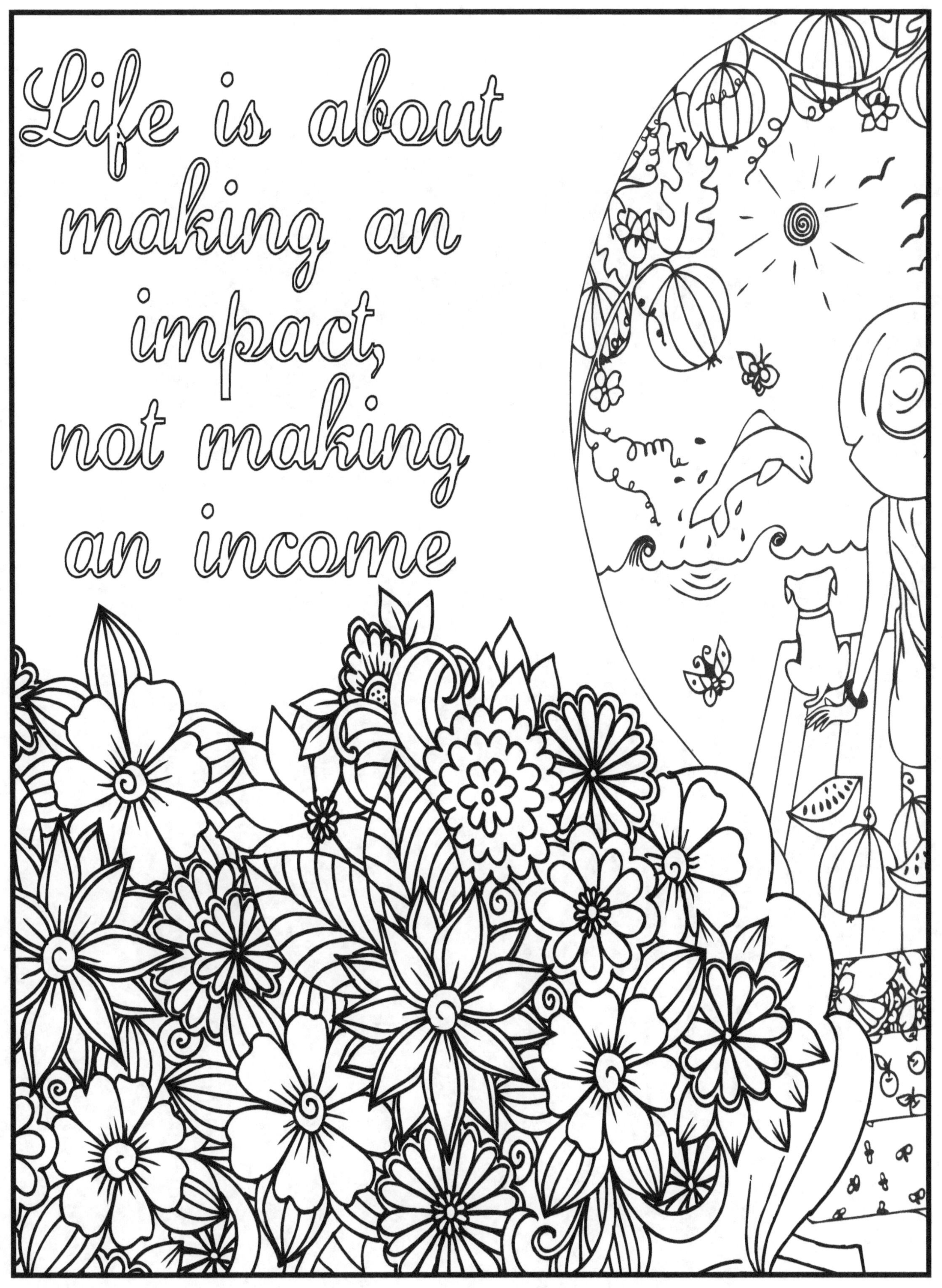

Life is about
making an
impact,
not making
an income

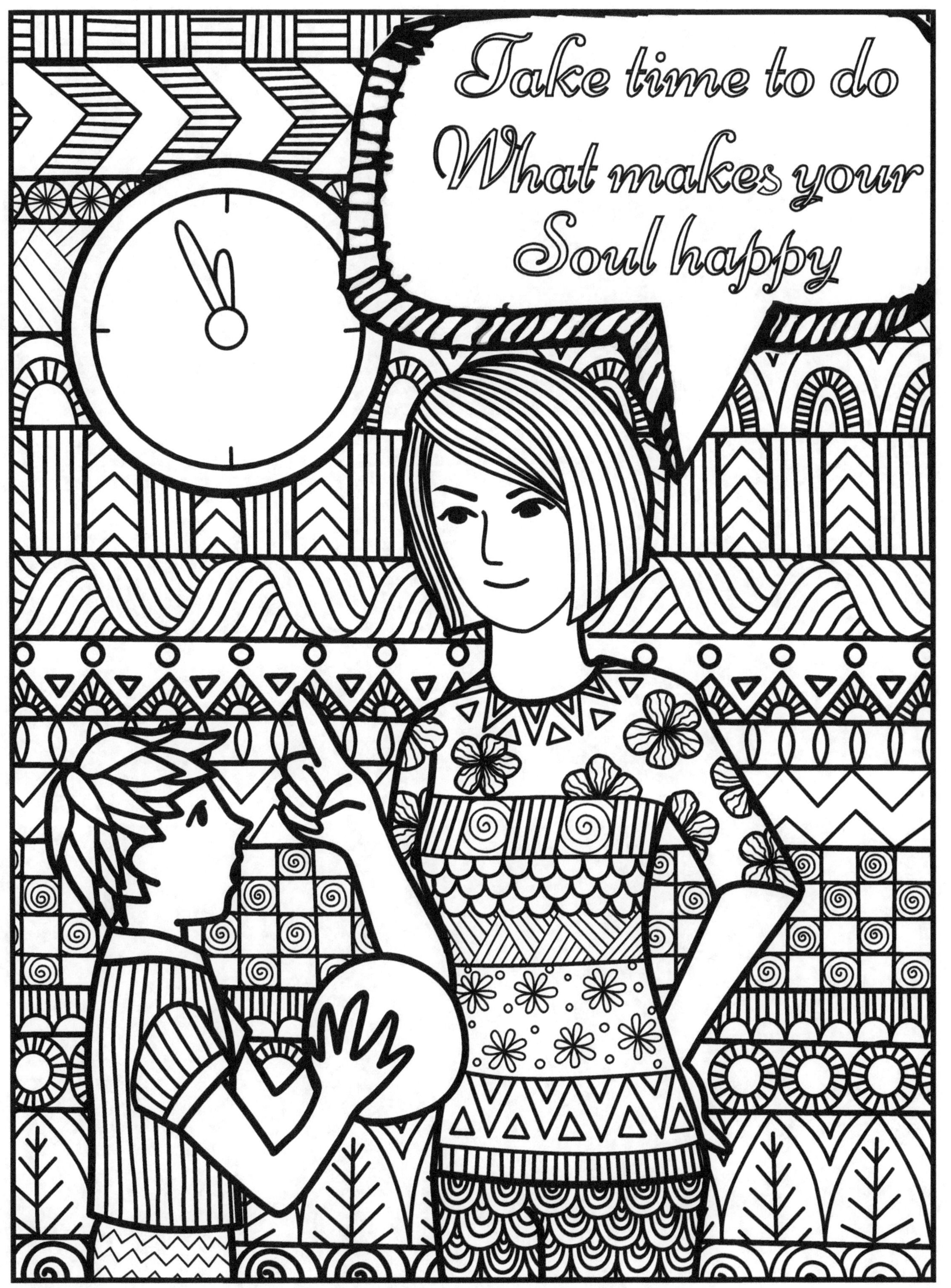

Take time to do
What makes your
Soul happy

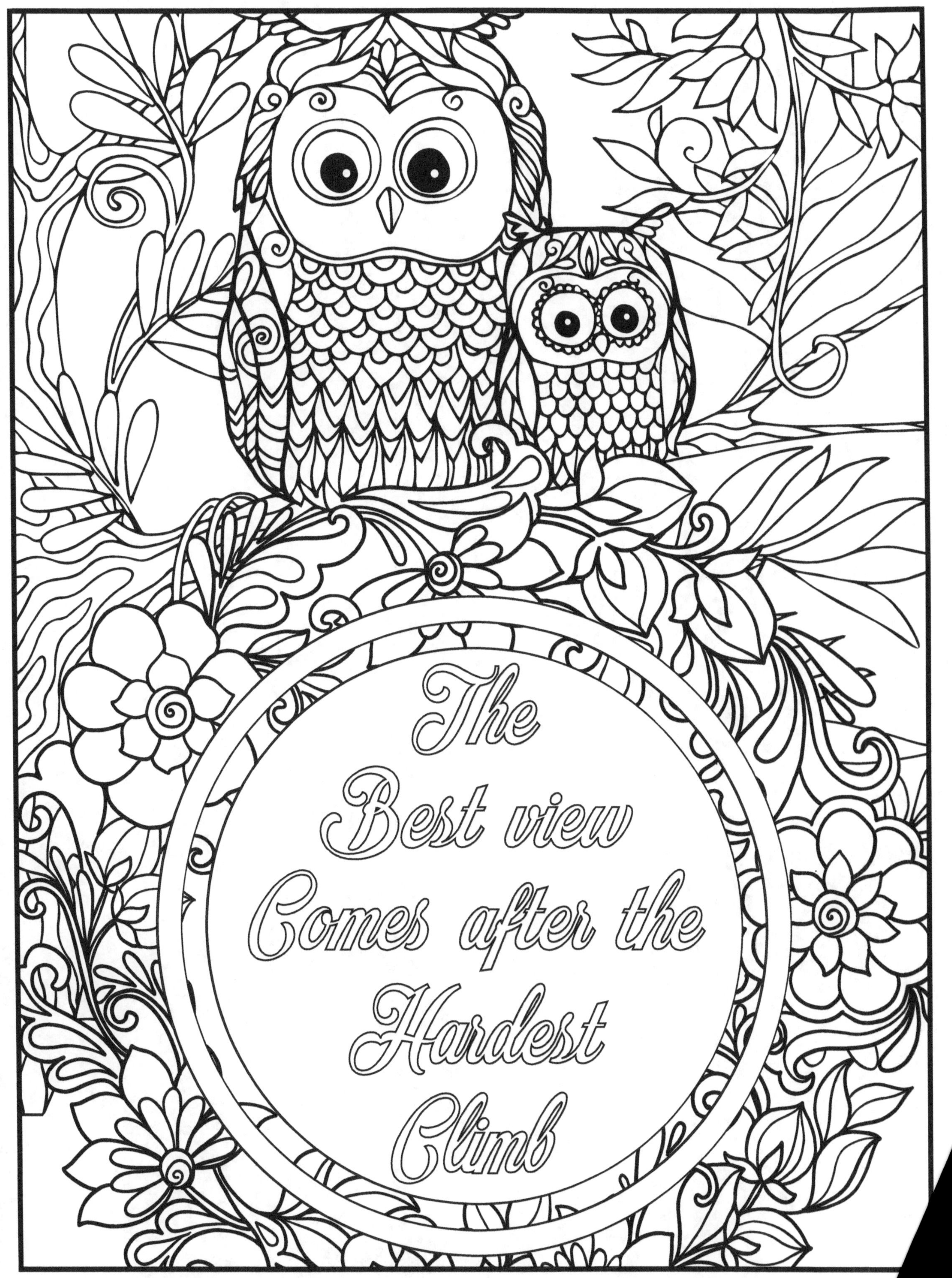

The
Best view
Comes after the
Hardest
Climb

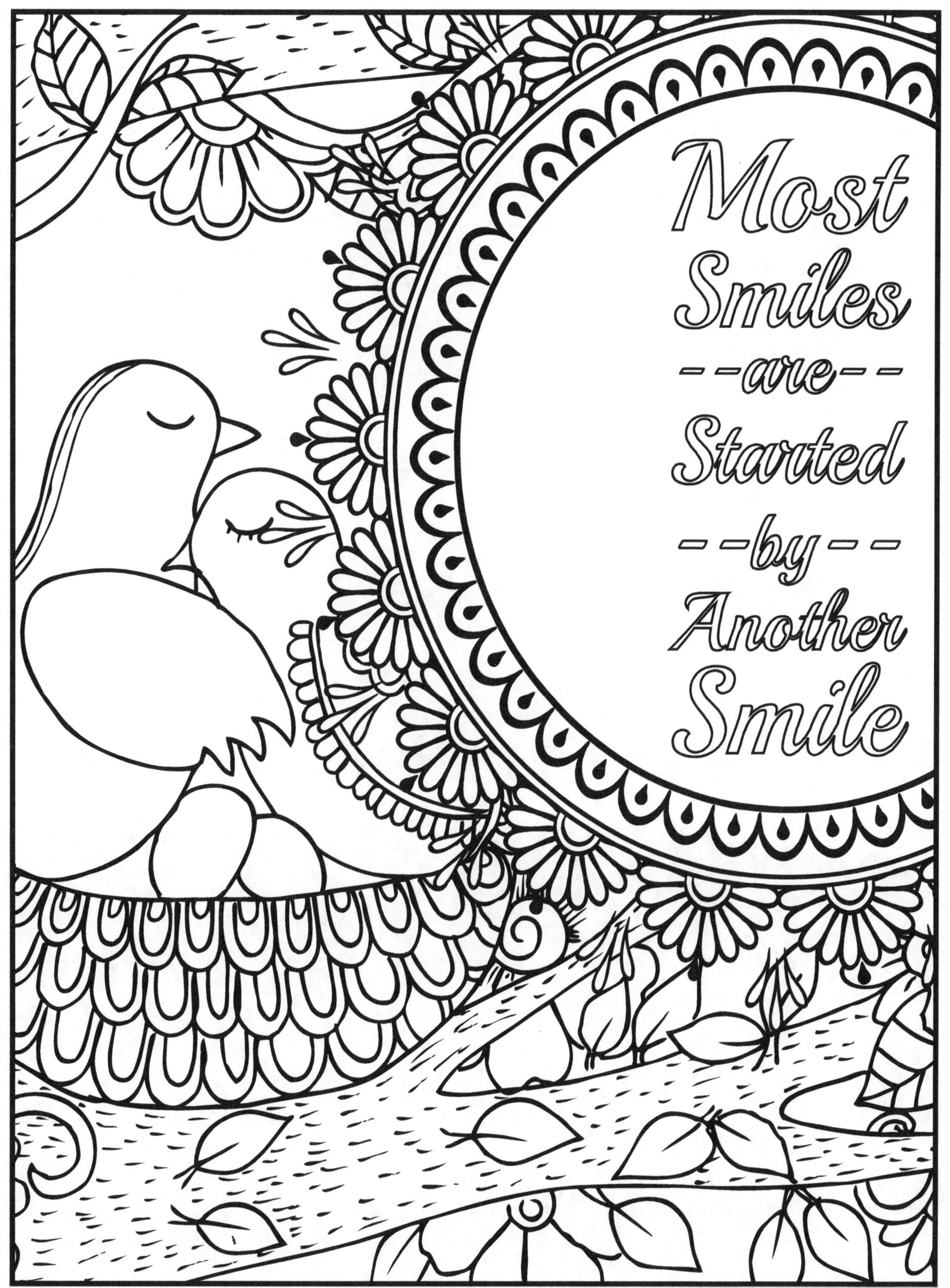

Most
Smiles
--are--
Started
--by--
Another
Smile

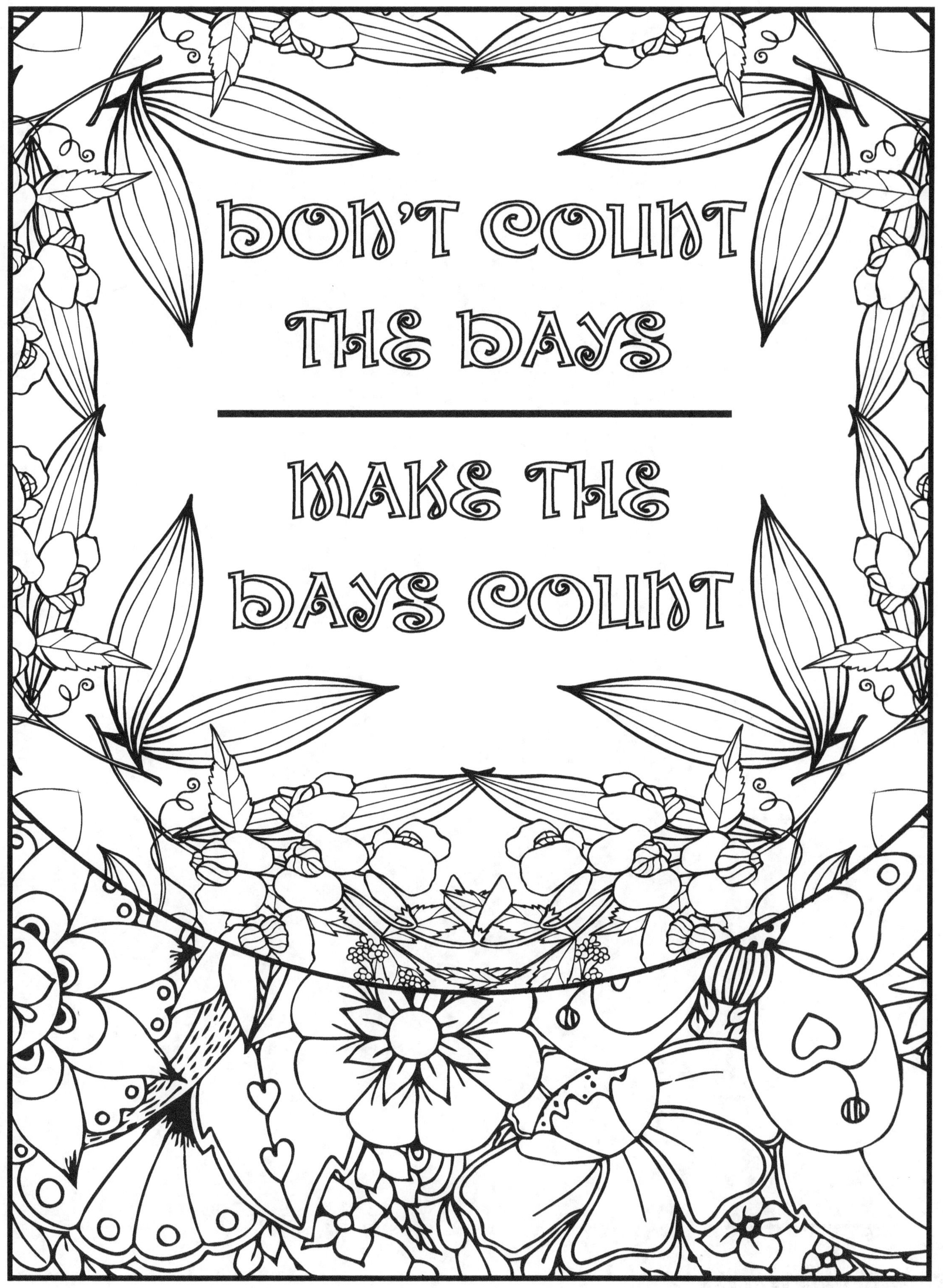

DON'T COUNT
THE DAYS
MAKE THE
DAYS COUNT